Charles H. Gabriel

Salvation Songs

For Gospel Meetings, Endeavor Societies, Epworth Leagues, Baptist Unions, Sunday Schools and Prayer Meetings

Charles H. Gabriel

Salvation Songs
For Gospel Meetings, Endeavor Societies, Epworth Leagues, Baptist Unions, Sunday Schools and Prayer Meetings

ISBN/EAN: 9783337182090

Printed in Europe, USA, Canada, Australia, Japan

Cover: Foto ©Thomas Meinert / pixelio.de

More available books at **www.hansebooks.com**

— FOR —

GOSPEL MEETINGS, ENDEAVOR SOCIETIES, EPWORTH
LEAGUES, BAPTIST UNIONS, SUNDAY SCHOOLS
AND PRAYER MEETINGS.

By CHAS. H. GABRIEL.

FILLMORE BROS.

119 W. SIXTH STREET,   NO. 40 BIBLE HOUSE,
CINCINNATI, O.   NEW YORK.

Copyright, 1895, by Fillmore Bros.

GREETING.

While a majority of the songs contained herein are new, and are now presented for the first time, among them will be found many of the prime favorites of the day, together with a few of the time-honored hymns and tunes of our fore-fathers; and if, thus mixed together, the old and the new assimilate and are found congenial companions, then SALVATION SONGS will become a joy alike to the young and to the old in the church.

In the regular service of the Church, Sunday School and the Prayer Meeting, as in the work of the Evangelist, the power and effect of special music (Solos, Duets, Quartets, etc.) has been demonstrated. Those contained herein will be found, in addition to their special uses, to be acceptable for congregational worship, and prove very useful to the Chorister.

As Solos, Nos. 11, 52, 109, 115, 122, 164, 208, and others, may be used; Nos. 116, 137, 171, and others, will be acceptable as Duets for Tenor (or Soprano) and Alto; any of the following numbers may be rendered as a Solo and Chorus: 42, 48, 66, 128, 160, 164. Among such as are suited for Duet and Chorus are Nos. 28, 34, 116, 182. Mixed Quartets will find use for Nos. 16, 19, 44, 84, 94, 102, 148, 175, 201, while Male Quartets will welcome Nos. 124, 146, 156 and 185.

Some of the short pieces will prove to be the choicest gems in the book, as nothing has been put in merely to fill out pages.

CHAS. H. GABRIEL.

CHICAGO, ILL., MARCH, 1895.

NOTICE.—Almost every one of the songs contained in this book, either the words or music, or both, or the arrangement of one or the other, or both, is copyright property, and must not be reproduced in any manner or duplicated by any process, without the written permission of the owner of the copyright, as such is an infringement, and amenable to the law.

THE PUBLISHERS.

ARMSTRONG & FILLMORE,
MUSIC TYPOGRAPHERS AND PRESS,
CINCINNATI, OHIO.

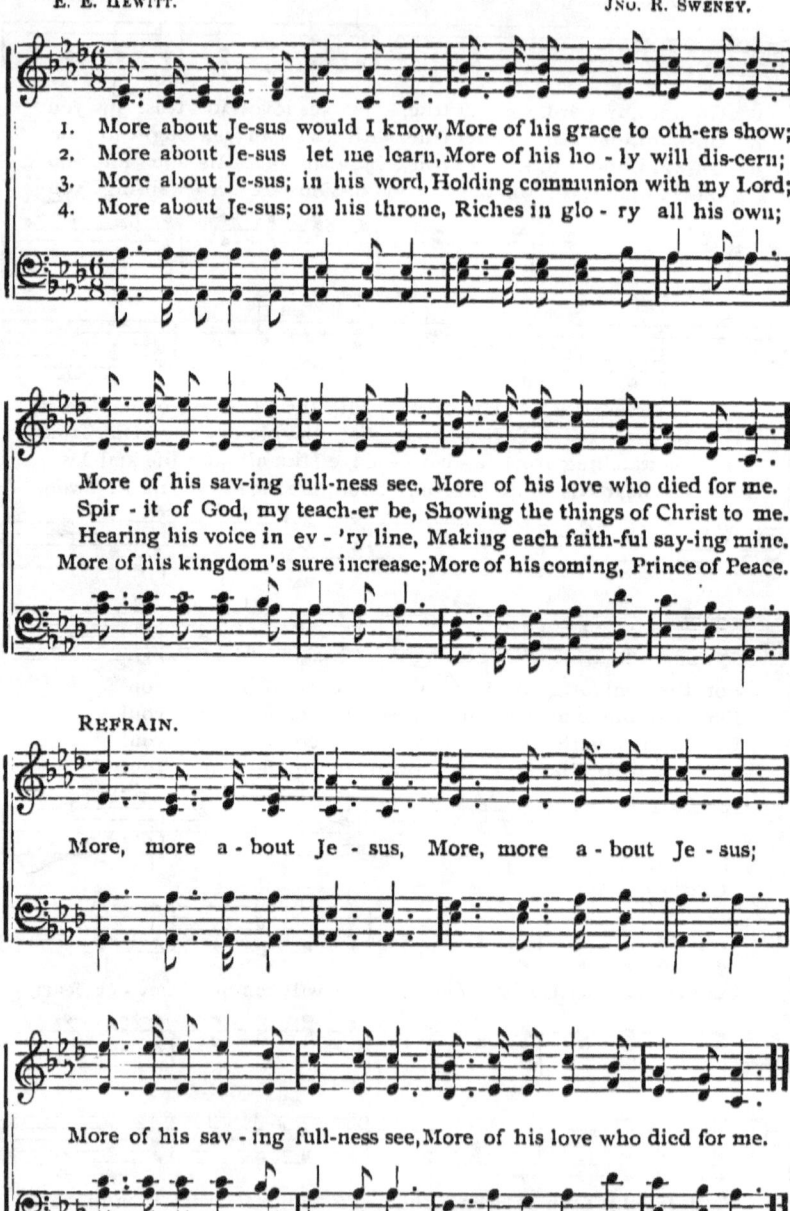

No. 9. THE VERY SAME JESUS.

L. H. Edmunds.   Wm. J. Kirkpatrick.

1. Come, sinners, to the Living One, He's just the same Jesus
2. Come, feast upon the "living bread," He's just the same Jesus
3. Come, tell him all your griefs and fears, He's just the same Jesus
4. Come, unto him for clearer light, He's just the same Jesus

As when he raised the widow's son, The very same Jesus.
As when the multitudes he fed, The very same Jesus.
As when he shed those loving tears, The very same Jesus.
As when he gave the blind their sight, The very same Jesus.

CHORUS.

The very same Jesus, The wonder working Jesus;

Oh, praise his name, he's just the same, The very same Jesus.

5. Calm 'midst the waves of trouble be,
He's just the same Jesus
As when he hush'd the raging sea,
The very same Jesus.

6. Some day our raptured eyes shall see
He's just the same Jesus;
Oh, blessed day for you and me!
The very same Jesus.

COPYRIGHT, 1891, BY WM. J. KIRKPATRICK. BY PER.

No. 10. SCATTER GOLDEN GRAIN.

ADA BLENKHORN. CHAS. H. GABRIEL.

1. 'Tis the time of sow-ing, and the day grows late! Fields of rich-est
2. Tell the bro-ken hearted Christ can make them whole! To the liv-ing
3. Doth thy wea-ry spir-it fal-ter by the way? Cloud and storm and
4. From the dawn of morn-ing till the close of day, Seeds of truth and

prom-ise for Thy com-ing wait; In the qui-et val-ley, o-ver
foun-tains lead the thirst-y soul; Wipe the tears of care and sor-row,
darkness oft ob-scure the day? Free-ly tell it all to Je-sus,
kind-ness scat-ter by the way; At the time of reap-ing, great in-

hill and o-ver plain, For the af-ter-reaping scat-ter gold-en grain.
tears that fall like rain, For the af-ter-reaping scat-ter gold-en grain.
He will soothe thy pain, For the af-ter-reaping scat-ter gold-en grain.
deed will be the gain, For the af-ter-reaping scat-ter gold-en grain.

CHORUS.

Scat-ter the grain, .. scat-ter the gold-en grain, When the
Scat-ter the gold-en grain, yes, scat-ter the gold-en grain,

sun is shining, when descends the rain, ... Scatter the gold-en grain,
descends the rain Scatter the golden grain,

COPYRIGHT, 1895, BY CHAS. H. GABRIEL.

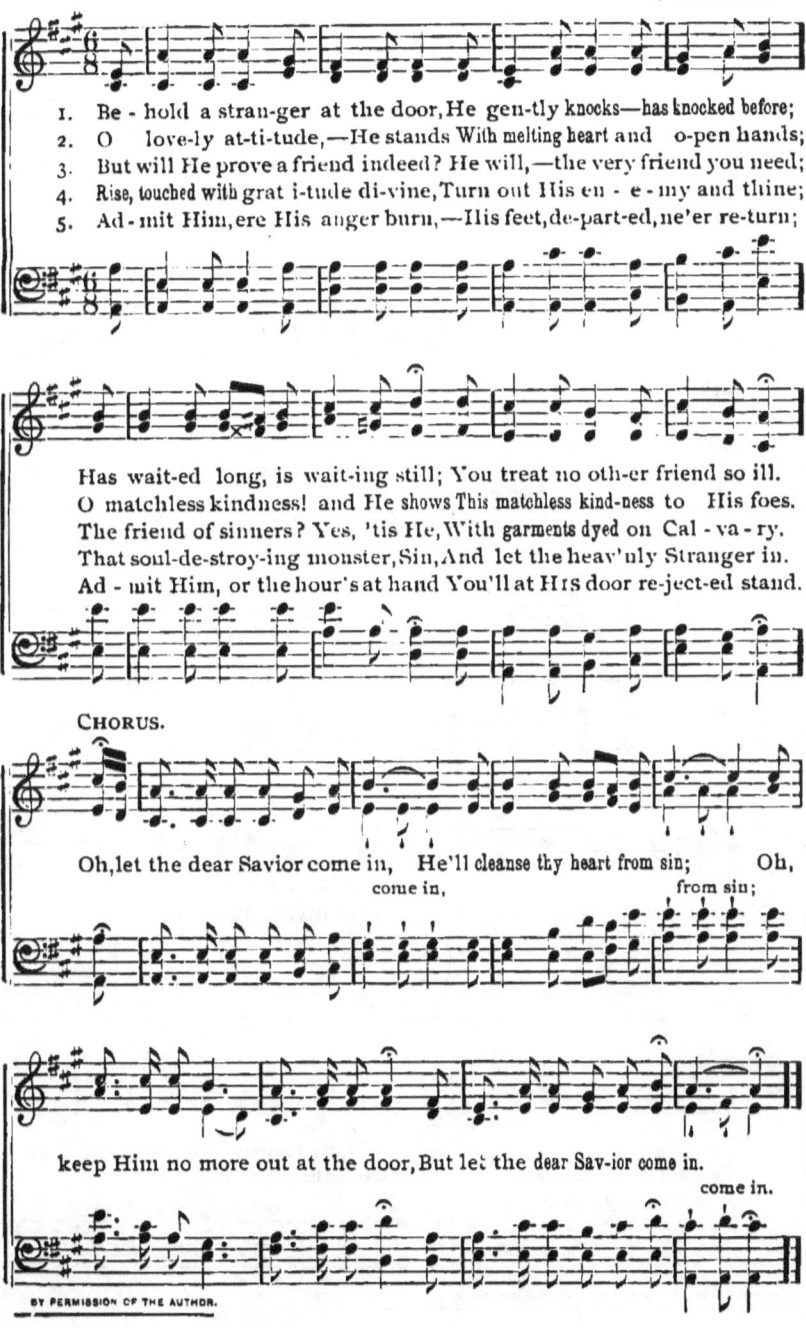

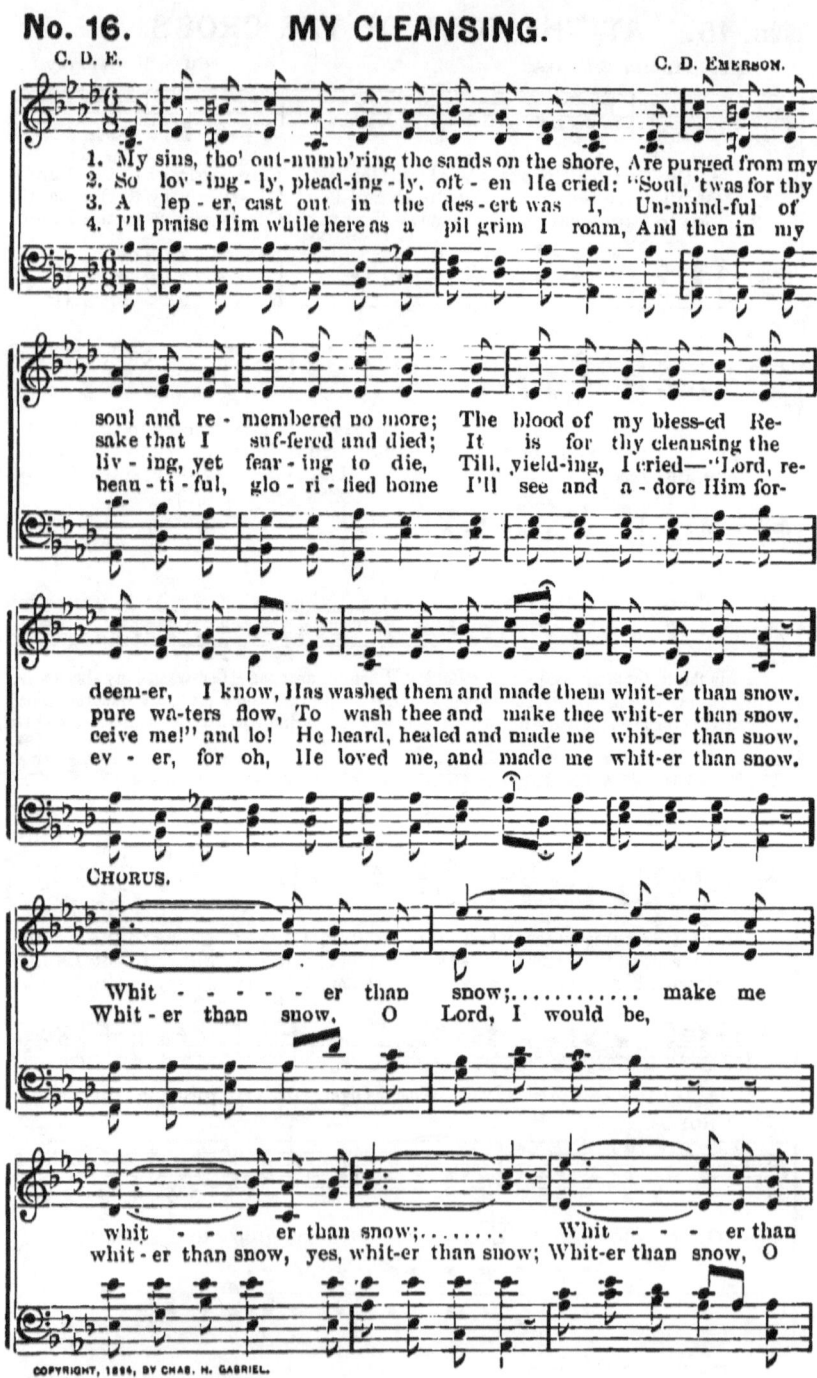

No. 18. THERE IS GLORY IN MY SOUL.

Mrs. Grace Weiser Davis.   Chas. H. Gabriel.

1. Since I lost my sins, and I found my Sav-ior, There is glo-ry
2. Since He cleansed my heart, and gave love's blest fullness, There is glo-ry
3. Since I walk with God hav-ing sweet com-mun-ion, There is glo-ry
4. I have entered Canaan on my way to heav-en, There is glo-ry

in my soul! Since I lost my bur-den and found God's fa-vor, There is
in my soul! Since He keeps me ful - ly in lov-ing kind-ness, There is
in my soul! Brighter grows each day in this heav'nly un-ion, There is
in my soul! And I claim as mine all my God has giv - en, There is

Chorus.

glo-ry in my soul. Yes, there's glory, glo-ry, there is glo-ry in my soul!

Ev-'ry day brighter grows, And I conquer all my foes; There is glo - ry,

glo-ry, yes, there's glory in my soul, There is glo-ry in my soul!

Copyright, 1894, by Chas. H. Gabriel.

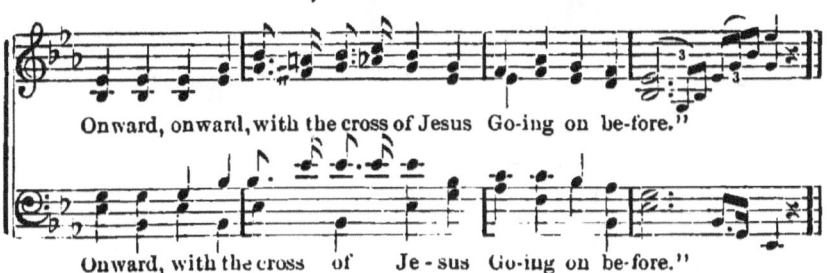

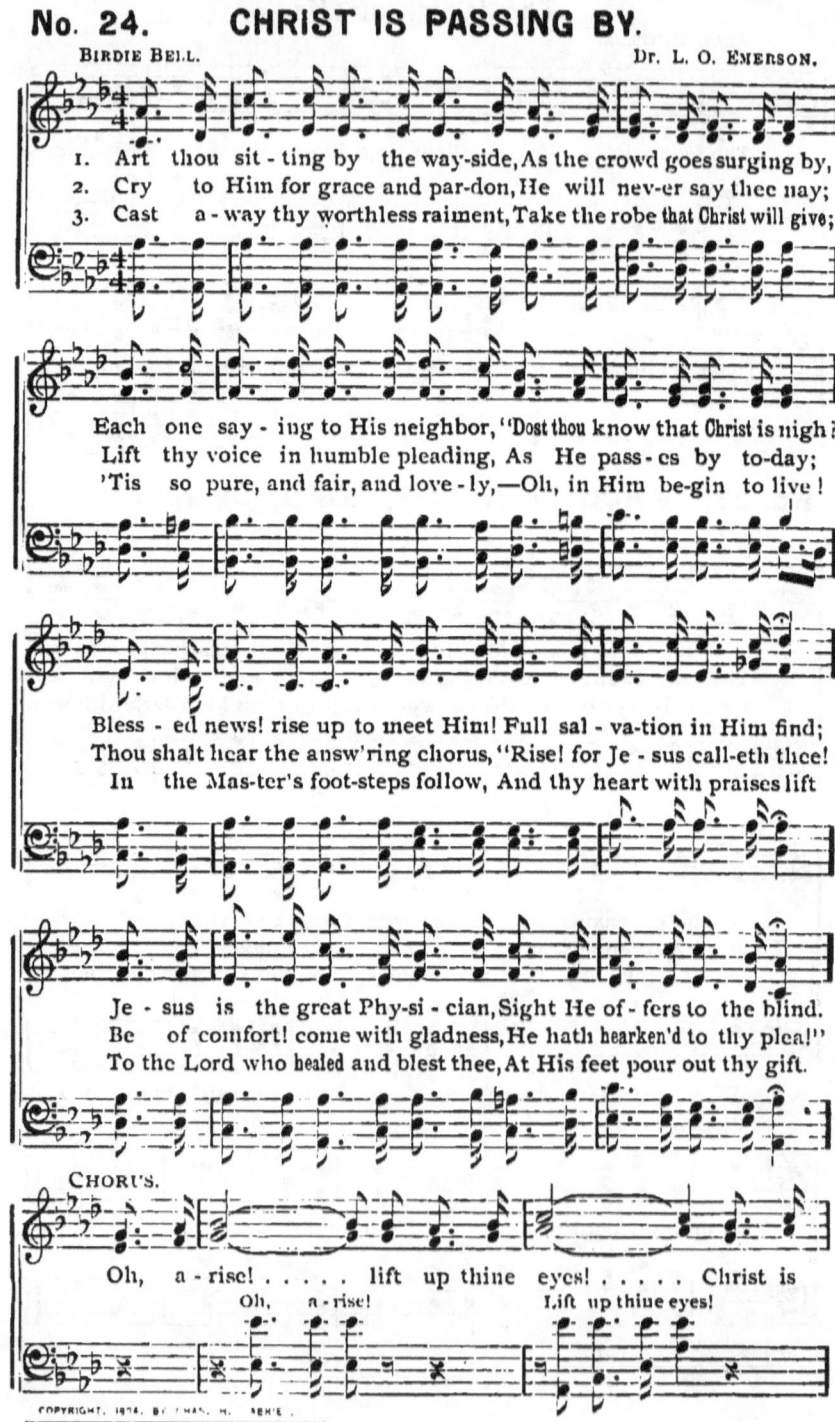

Christ is Passing By.

pass - - ing by to-day! . . . . He will heal . .
Christ is pass-ing, pass-ing by to-day! He will heal

thee, He will save thee, Ere He pass - - es by to-day.
thee, He will save thee, Ere He pass-es by to-day.

rit.

No. 25. COME THOU, O TRAVELER.

J. E. RANKIN, D. D. CHAS. H. GABRIEL.

1. Come thou, O trav-'ler blest, Seek-ing to be a guest
2. Spread thou the Pas-chal feast; From E-gypt's bonds re-leased,
3. Tem-ple, hence-forth, of Thine, Mark'd by Thy lin-tel sign,

With-in my soul; My heart, oppressed and sore, Throws o-pen
Come, sup with me; On Thee I lean my head, Break Thou the
Sprin-kled with blood; Loins gird-ed now I stand. Faith's staff with-

wide the door; Welcome for-ev-er-more: Take full con-trol.
liv-ing bread, Pour Thou the wine once shed On Cal-va-ry.
in my hand, To cross to Canaan's land, Death's an-gry flood.

COPYRIGHT, 1894, BY CHAS. H. GABRIEL.

No. 27. THIS LOST WORLD FOR JESUS.

Rev. J. E. Rankin, D. D.   Chas. H. Gabriel.

1. This lost, lost world for Je-sus! 'Twas heav'n He put a-side; On earth He walked in-car-nate, Was scourged and cru-ci-fied; Then let the King Im-man-uel, Who left for us a throne, Re-turn and take pos-sess-ion, Re-turn and claim His own.

2. This lost, lost world for Je-sus! From where the ris-ing sun Lights up the o-rient mount-ain To where his course is run; He is the world's re-deem-er! Let all be-neath the skies Speak back to Him one language In praise and sac-ri-fice.

3. This lost, lost world for Je-sus! He comes to make it bloom, Be read-y for the sig-nal, Pre-pare His kingdom room; A King's a-bout a-mong us! Be this our bat-tle call: "This lost, lost world for Je-sus, He well de-serves it all."

Chorus.

This lost, lost world for Je-sus, This world (lost world) for Je-sus; This lost, lost world for Je-sus, This world (lost world) for Je-sus.

Copyright, 1891, by Chas. H. Gabriel.

No. 30. THE PRECIOUS BLOOD.

Rev. J. M. ORROCK.   CHAS. H. GABRIEL.

1. To Cal-va-ry, O sinner, come, Come burden'd with your sin and shame;
2. To Joseph's tomb, O sinner, come, The bur-ied Savior triumphs there;
3. To heav-en now, O sin-ner, look, The ris-en Je-sus there appears;

Up-on the cross there hangeth One, Em-man-u-el His bless-ed name.
His res-ur-rec-tion proves that He Was chos-en all our sins to bear.
He pleads His death up-on the cross, And pen-i-tents may dry their tears.

CHORUS.

Oh, see His blood, the precious blood! The blood of the in-car-nate God!

'Twas shed for you, 'twas shed for me, That from our sin we might be free.

COPYRIGHT, 1894, BY CHAS. H. GABRIEL.

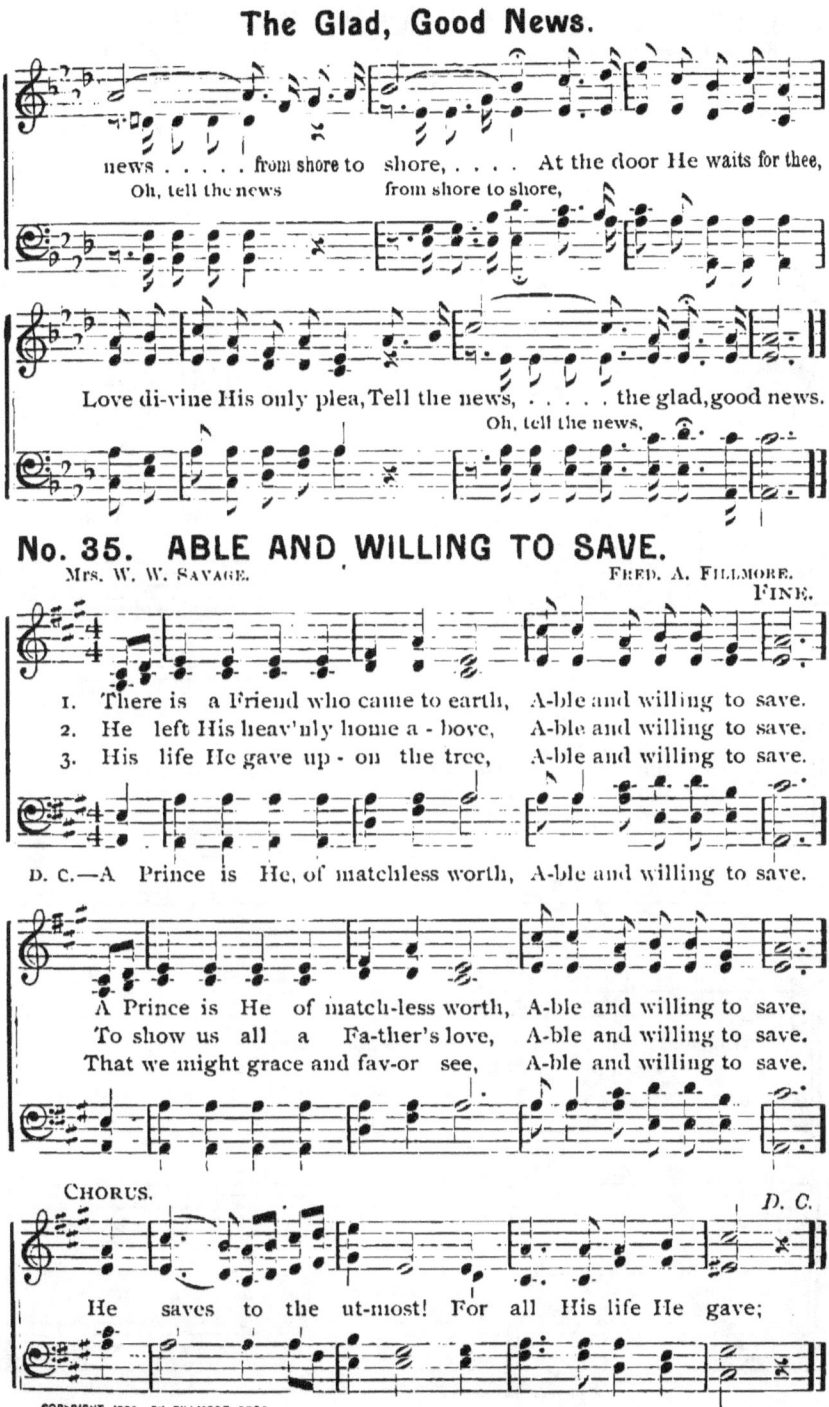

No. 41. BLESSED ASSURANCE.

Fanny J. Crosby.
Mrs. J. F. Knapp.

1. Bless-ed as-sur-ance, Je-sus is mine! Oh, what a fore-taste of glo-ry di-vine! Heir of sal-va-tion, purchased of God, Born of His Spir-it, wash'd in His blood.
2. Per-fect sub-mis-sion, Per-fect de-light, Vis-ions of rapt-ure now burst on my sight, An-gels de-scend-ing, bring from a-bove, Ech-oes of mer-cy, whis-pers of love.
3. Per-fect sub-mis-sion, All is at rest, I, in my Sav-ior, am hap-py and blest, Watch-ing and wait-ing, look-ing a-bove, Filled with His goodness, lost in His love.

CHORUS.

This is my sto-ry, this is my song, Praising my Sav-ior all the day long: This is my sto-ry, this is my song, Prais-ing my Sav-ior all the day long.

Copyright, 1873, by Jos. F. Knapp.

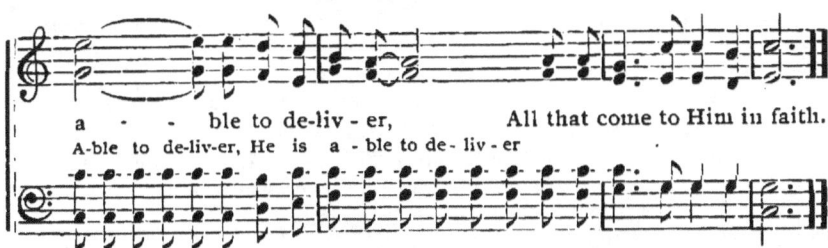

No. 45. AS THY DAYS THY STRENGTH SHALL BE.

Wm. F. Lloyd.   Rev. J. M. Driver.

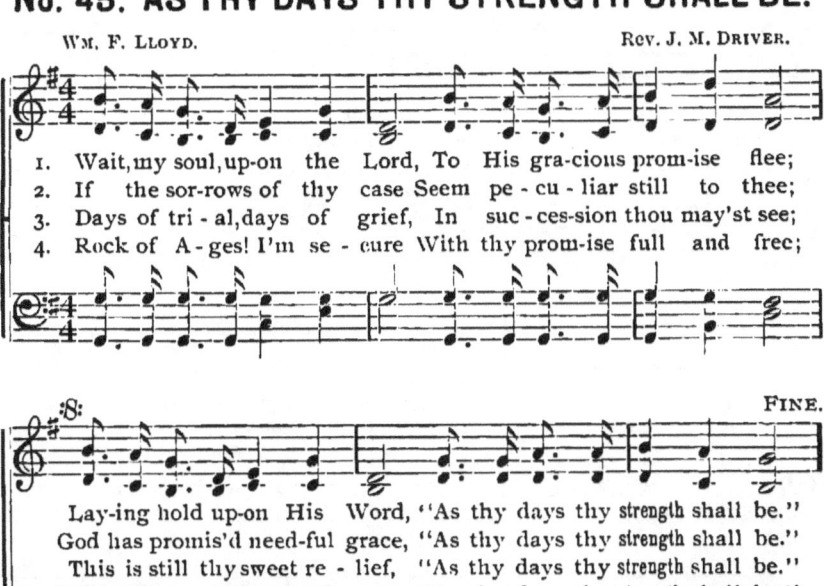

1. Wait, my soul, up-on the Lord, To His gra-cious prom-ise flee;
2. If the sor-rows of thy case Seem pe-cu-liar still to thee;
3. Days of tri-al, days of grief, In suc-ces-sion thou may'st see;
4. Rock of A-ges! I'm se-cure With thy prom-ise full and free;

Lay-ing hold up-on His Word, "As thy days thy strength shall be."
God has promis'd need-ful grace, "As thy days thy strength shall be."
This is still thy sweet re-lief, "As thy days thy strength shall be."
Faith-ful, pos-i-tive and sure— "As thy days thy strength shall be."

D.S.—This is still thy sweet re-lief, "As thy days thy strength shall be."

Chorus.   D. S.

"As thy days thy strength shall be:" "As thy days thy strength shall be;"

BY PERMISSION OF THE AUTHOR.

No. 46. JOY OF CONSECRATION.

MAGGIE E. GREGORY. Dr. S. B. JACKSON.

1. What blessed peace the tho't affords When we can say we're all the Lord's!
2. What joy it is our Lord to serve, When we are His with-out re-serve!
3. To Thee, dear Christ, our wills we bring, Thy love we mag-ni-fy and sing,

And when in con-se-cra-tion sweet, Our wills are laid at Je-sus' feet.
When we can say from in-most soul, His blood doth make us fully whole.
And feel what joy the tho't affords, Since we can say we're all the Lord's

CHORUS.

Be-yond the fear of grief and pain, To live is
Christ, to die is gain, Cleansed are our hearts from sin and
car-nal pride, When we with Christ are cru-ci-fied.

COPYRIGHT, 1895, BY CHAS. H. GABRIEL.

No. 47. ON THE ROCK.

FRED WOODROW. C. C. CASE.

1. Standing on the Rock of A-ges, The Rock that shall en-dure, Un-shak-en by
2. Standing on the Rock of A-ges, We view the tranquil soul, Untroubled by
3. Standing on the Rock of A-ges, No need have we to fear, God ban-ish-es

the tem-pest, E-ter-nal, firm and sure; There is a safe re-treat, A
the tem-pest, Or surg-ing billows' roll; Be dangers what they may, And
our sor-row, God wipes a-way our tear; We're watching, we believe, We

refuge strong and free, A-mid the stormy billows Of life's tempestuous sea.
break the waves of care, A-mid the wild com-mo-tion, We stand in safe-ty there.
trust His promise sure, That crowns of joy are wait-ing For all His saints se-cure.

CHORUS.

Stand - - ing, stand - ing, Standing on the Rock of A-ges,
Standing on the Rock, I am standing on the Rock.

Stand - - ing, stand - - ing, No need have I to fear.
Standing on the Rock, I am standing on the Rock,

COPYRIGHT, 1893, BY CHAS. H. GABRIEL.

No. 50. THE MASTER IS CALLING.

Mrs. Harriet E. Jones.   Chas. H. Gabriel.

1. My broth-er, the Mas-ter is call-ing for thee, Call-ing for thee, He is call-ing for thee; The full-ness of rich-es He of-fers you free,—He's call-ing for thee, for thee; He lov-ing-ly, ten-der-ly calls you to-day, O will you ac-cept Him? how can you de-lay!

2. The Mas-ter is call-ing, O make Him your choice; Call-ing for thee, He is call-ing for thee; If you will accept Him, your soul will re-joice,—He's call-ing for thee, for thee; He's wait-ing so pa-tient-ly now to re-ceive; O fly to Him, brother, look up and be-lieve.

3. The Mas-ter is call-ing, the Mas-ter who gave—Call-ing for thee, He is call-ing for thee; His life for the sin-ner, the might-y to save,—He's call-ing for thee, for thee; Ac-cept Him, my broth-er, get un-der the blood, Be white as the snow thro' the soul-cleansing flood.

Chorus.

Call - - ing for thee, He's call - - ing for
Call-ing for thee, He's call-ing for thee, the Mas-ter is call-ing, is

Copyright, 1895, by Chas. H. Gabriel.

The Master is Calling.

thee! ... O haste to His feet and in pen-i-tence bow. For He's
call-ing for thee!

call - - ing now; ... Call - - ing for
call-ing He's call-ing thee now, just now; Call-ing for thee, He is

thee, ... He is call - - ing for thee .... So
call-ing for thee, The Mas-ter is call-ing, is call-ing for thee, So

lov-ing-ly, ten-der-ly call - - ing for thee. .....
lov - ing-ly, ten - der-ly call-ing, He's call-ing for thee, for thee.

No. 51. MY FAITH LOOKS UP TO THEE.

1 My faith looks up to Thee,
　Thou Lamb of Calvary,
　　Savior divine;
　Now hear me while I pray:
　Take all my guilt away;
　O let me from this day
　　Be wholly thine.

2 May Thy rich grace impart
　Strength to my fainting heart;
　　My zeal inspire;

As Thou hast died for me,
O may my love to Thee
Pure, warm and changeless be,
　A living fire.

3 While life's dark maze I tread,
　And griefs around me spread,
　　Be Thou my guide;
　Bid darkness turn to day;
　Wipe sorrow's tears away,
　Nor let me ever stray
　　From Thee away.

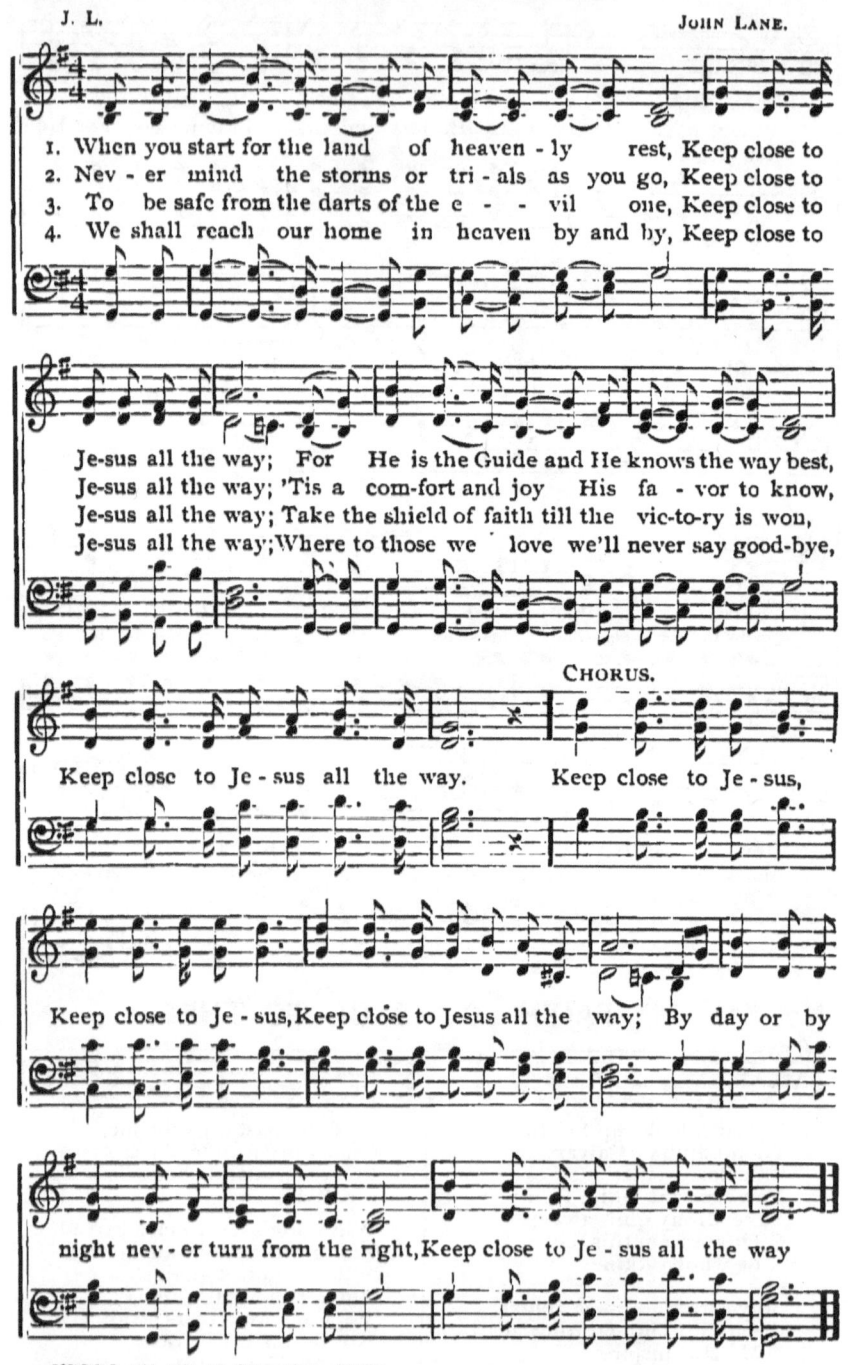

No. 53. SOWING AND REAPING.

E. E. Hewitt.   Chas. H. Gabriel.

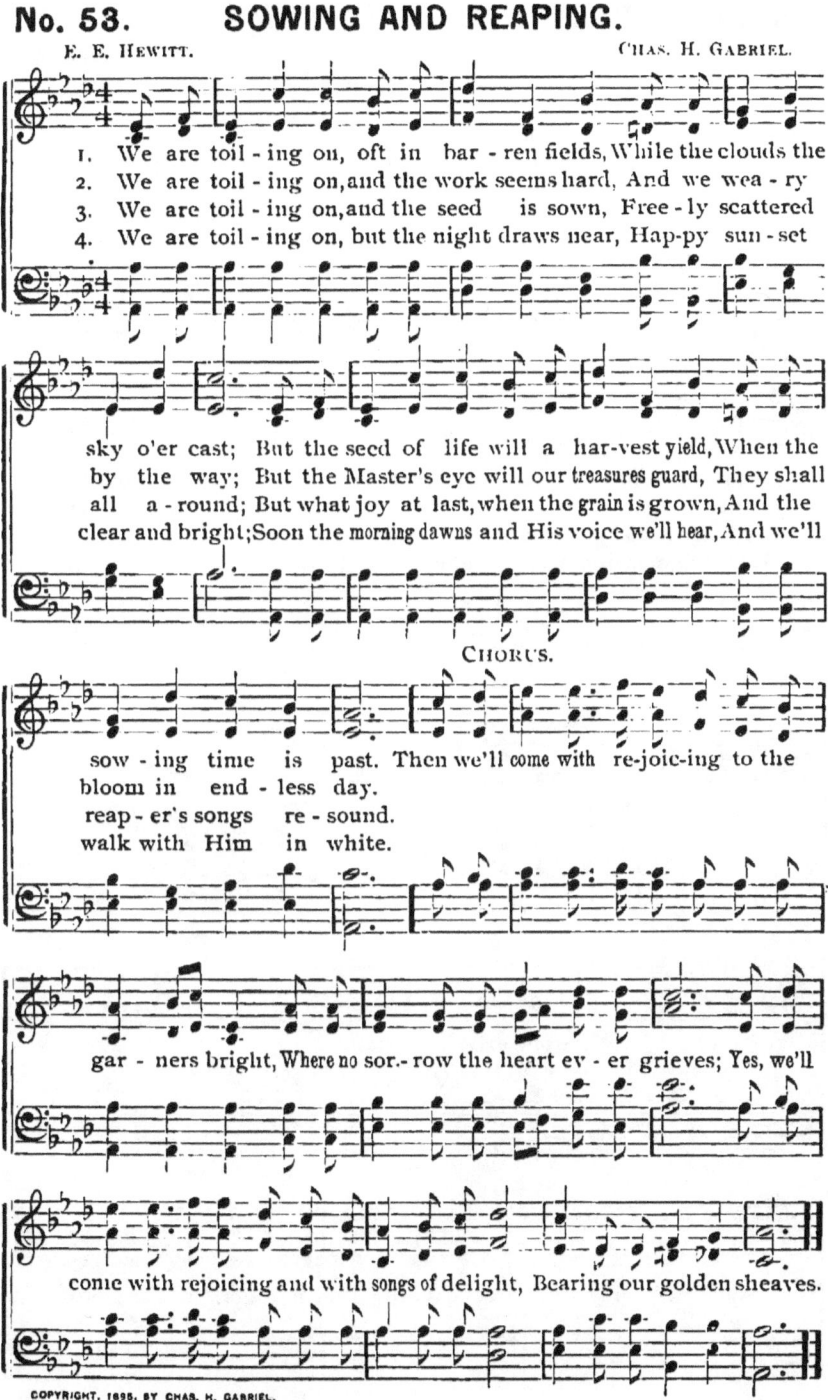

1. We are toil-ing on, oft in bar-ren fields, While the clouds the sky o'er cast; But the seed of life will a har-vest yield, When the sow-ing time is past.
2. We are toil-ing on, and the work seems hard, And we wea-ry by the way; But the Master's eye will our treasures guard, They shall bloom in end-less day.
3. We are toil-ing on, and the seed is sown, Free-ly scattered all a-round; But what joy at last, when the grain is grown, And the reap-er's songs re-sound.
4. We are toil-ing on, but the night draws near, Hap-py sun-set clear and bright; Soon the morning dawns and His voice we'll hear, And we'll walk with Him in white.

CHORUS.
Then we'll come with re-joic-ing to the gar-ners bright, Where no sor-row the heart ev-er grieves; Yes, we'll come with rejoicing and with songs of delight, Bearing our golden sheaves.

Copyright, 1895, by Chas. H. Gabriel.

No. 58. BRIGHT FOREVER.

GRACE J. FRANCES. HUBERT P. MAIN.

1. Breaking thro' the clouds that gath-er O'er the Christian's na-tal skies,
2. Yet a lit-tle while we lin-ger, Ere we reach our journey's end;
3. Oh, the bliss of life e-ter-nal! Oh! the long un-bro-ken rest!

Dis-tant beams, like floods of glo-ry, Fill the soul with glad sur-prise;
Yet a lit-tle while of la-bor, Ere the evening shades descend;
In the gold-en fields of pleasure, In the re-gion of the blest;

And we al-most hear the ech-o Of the pure and ho-ly throng,
Then we'll lay us down to slum-ber, But the night will soon be o'er;
But to see our dear Re-deem-er, And be-fore His throne to fall,

rit.

In the bright, the bright for-ev-er, In the sum-mer-land of song.
In the bright, the bright for-ev-er, We shall wake, to weep no more.
There to hear His gracious welcome—Will be sweet-er far than all.

CHORUS

On the banks beyond the riv-er, We shall meet, no more to sev-er;

COPYRIGHT, 1871, BY BIGLOW & MAIN. USED BY PER.

Bright Forever.

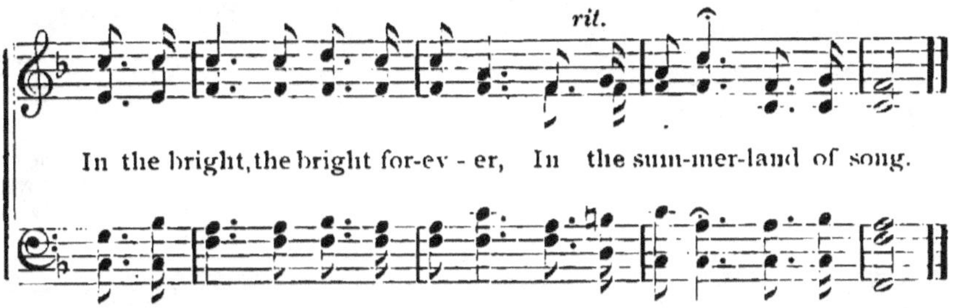

In the bright, the bright for-ev - er, In the sum-mer-land of song.

No. 59. MORE LOVE TO THEE, O CHRIST.

Mrs. E. Prentiss. Dr. W. H. Doane.

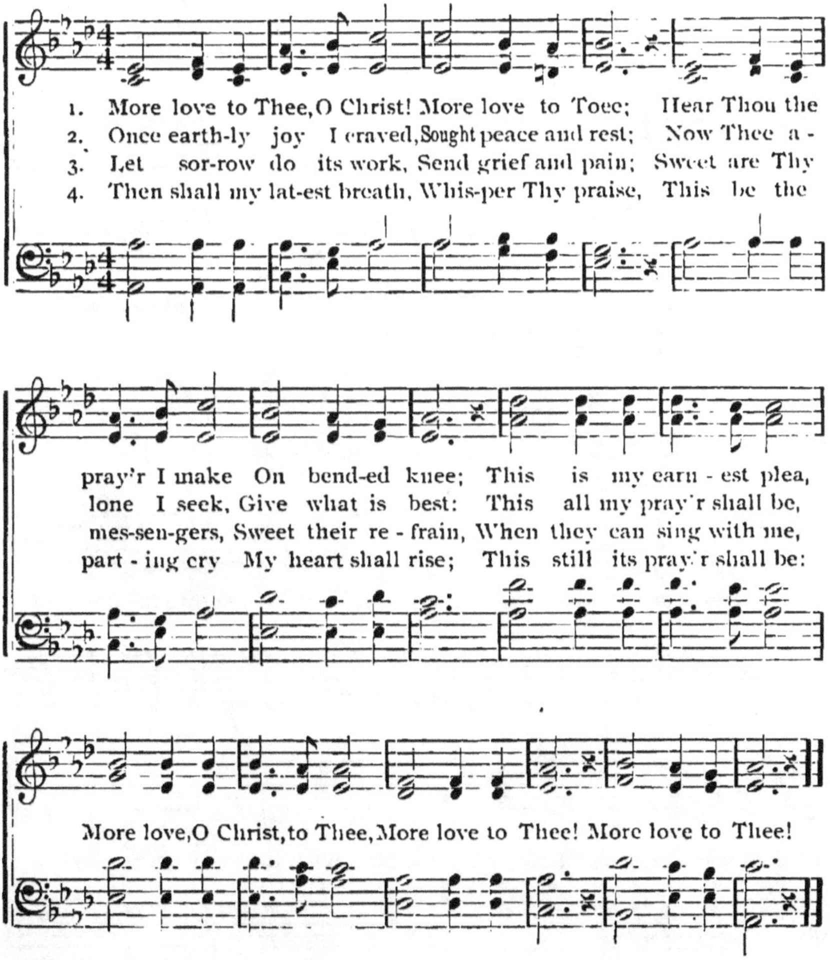

1. More love to Thee, O Christ! More love to Thee; Hear Thou the
2. Once earth-ly joy I craved, Sought peace and rest; Now Thee a-
3. Let sor-row do its work, Send grief and pain; Sweet are Thy
4. Then shall my lat-est breath, Whis-per Thy praise, This be the

pray'r I make On bend-ed knee; This is my earn - est plea,
lone I seek, Give what is best: This all my pray'r shall be,
mes-sen-gers, Sweet their re - frain, When they can sing with me,
part - ing cry My heart shall rise; This still its pray'r shall be:

More love, O Christ, to Thee, More love to Thee! More love to Thee!

COPYRIGHT, 1870, BY W. H. DOANE. USED BY PER.

Mercy is Boundless and Free.

D. C. *Refrain.*

Life ev-er-last-ing thy soul may receive, Mer-cy is boundless and free.
Je - sus is waiting, He'll save you to-night, Mer-cy is boundless and free.
Grieve Him no longer, but come as thou art, Mer-cy is boundless and free.
Cling to His mer-cy, be-lieve on His name, Mer-cy is boundless and free.

No. 65. GLORIOUS FOUNTAIN,

COWPER. T. C. O'KANE.

1. { There is a fountain filled with blood, filled with blood, filled with blood,
    And sinners, plung'd beneath that flood, be-neath that flood, beneath that flood,
2. { The dy - ing thief re-joiced to see, re-joiced to see, re-joiced to see,
    And there may I, tho' vile as he, tho' vile as he, tho' vile as he,

There is a fount-ain filled with blood, Drawn from Immanuel's veins, }
And sinners, plung'd beneath that flood, Lose all their guilt-y stains }
The dy - ing thief re-joiced to see That fount-ain in his day, }
And there may I, tho' vile as he, Wash all my sins a-way. }

CHORUS.

Oh, glo-ri-ous fount-ain! Here will I stay, And in thee ev - er Wash my sins a-way.

3 Thou dying Lamb. ‖: Thy precious blood, :‖
　Shall never lose its power,
　Till all the ransomed ‖: Church of God, :‖
　Are saved to sin no more.

4 E'er since by faith ‖: I saw the stream, :‖
　Thy flowing wounds supply,
　Redeeming love ‖: love has been my theme, :‖
　And shall be till I die.

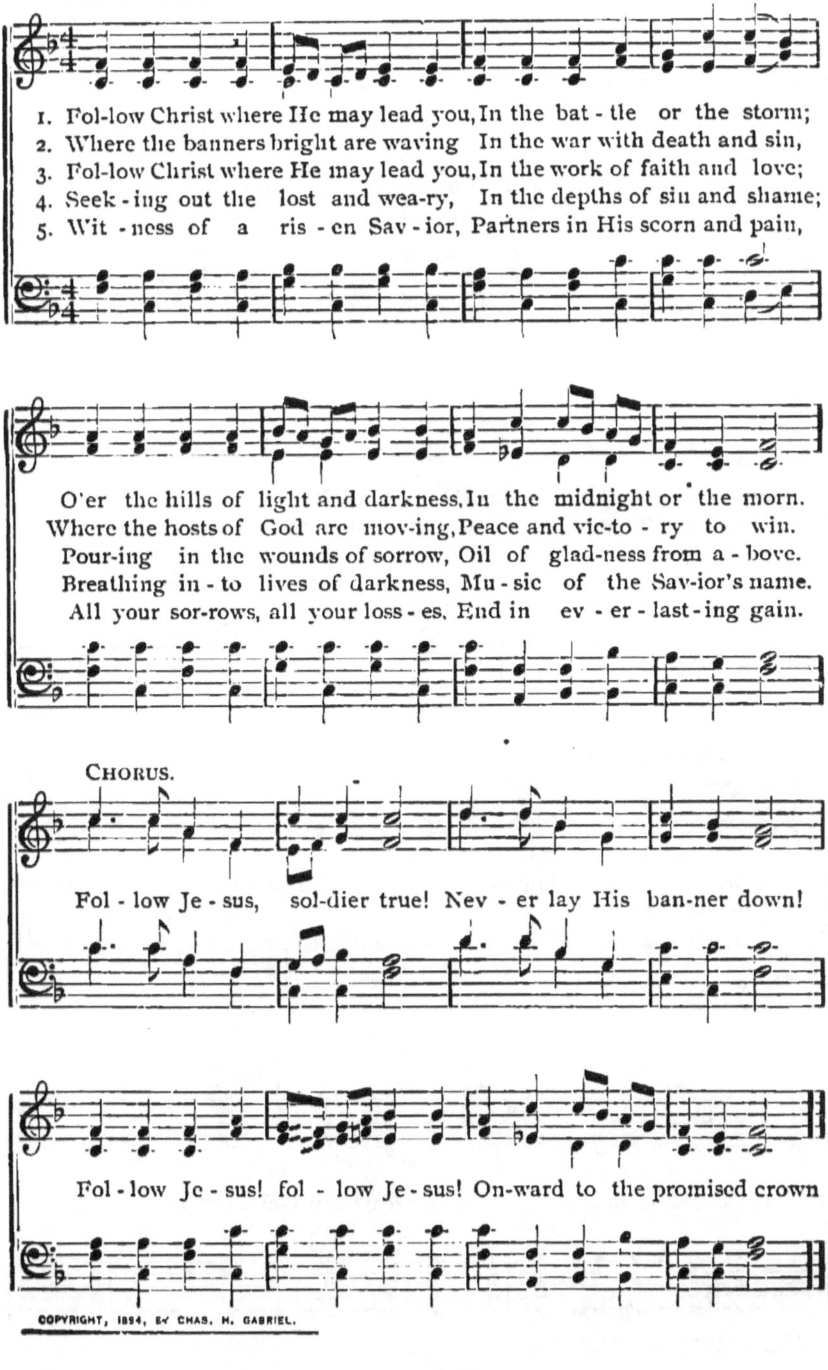

No. 68. I'M NOT ALONE.

MARY B. PECK. JOHN E. KURZENKNABE.

1. When dark'ning shadows 'round me fall, And light and hope seem gone,
2. His eye can pierce the darkest cloud, His arm all danger stay;
3. When sorrows come with crushing blow O'er my defenceless head,
4. So cheerfully I'll travel on Thro' life's dark, thorny way;

There is one tho't my heart upholds: It is, I'm not alone.
He waits for neither look nor word, Our troubles to allay.
I tremble not; for well I know Who by my side doth tread.
I'll fear no ill, I'm not alone, While Jesus is my stay.

CHORUS.

No, never alone, Can Jesus' followers be;
No, not alone,

He's ever near! why should we fear? Our Guide and Hope is He.

COPYRIGHT, BY J. H. KURZENKNABE.

No. 69. DRAW ME NEARER.

Fanny J. Crosby. Dr. W. H. Doane.

1. I am thine, O Lord, I have heard Thy voice, And it told Thy love to me;
2. Consecrate me now to Thy service, Lord, By the pow'r of grace di-vine;
3. Oh, the pure delight of a sin-gle hour That before Thy throne I spend,
4. There are depths of love that I cannot know Till I cross the nar-row sea,

But I long to rise in the arms of faith, And be closer drawn to Thee.
Let my soul look up with a steadfast hope, And my will be lost in Thine.
When I kneel in pray'r, and with Thee my God, I commune as friend with friend.
There are heights of joy that I may not reach Till I rest in peace with Thee.

Chorus.

Draw me near-er, near-er, blessed Lord, To the cross where Thou hast died;
near-er, near-er,

Draw me nearer, near-er, nearer, bless-ed Lord, To Thy precious bleeding side.

BY PER. OF W. H. DOANE, OWNER OF THE COPYRIGHT.

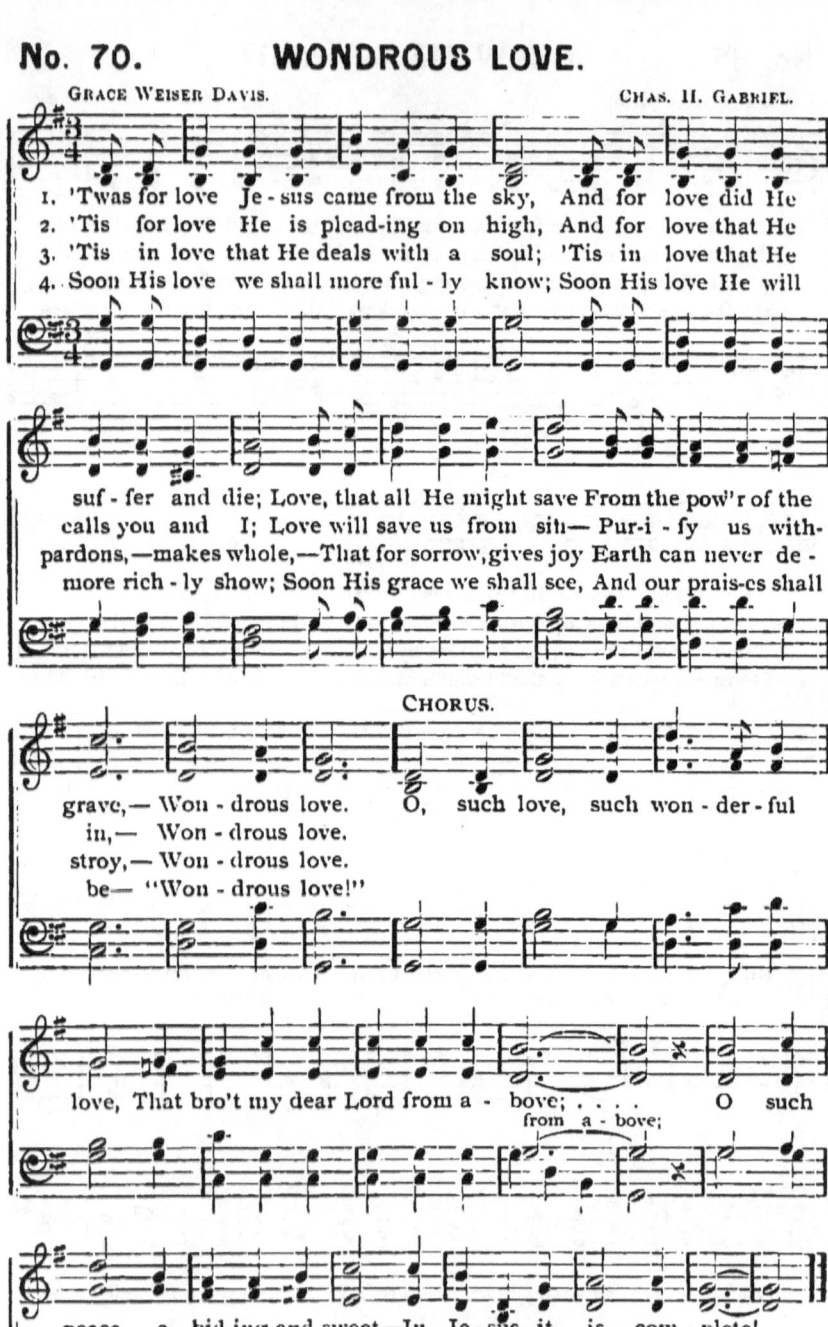

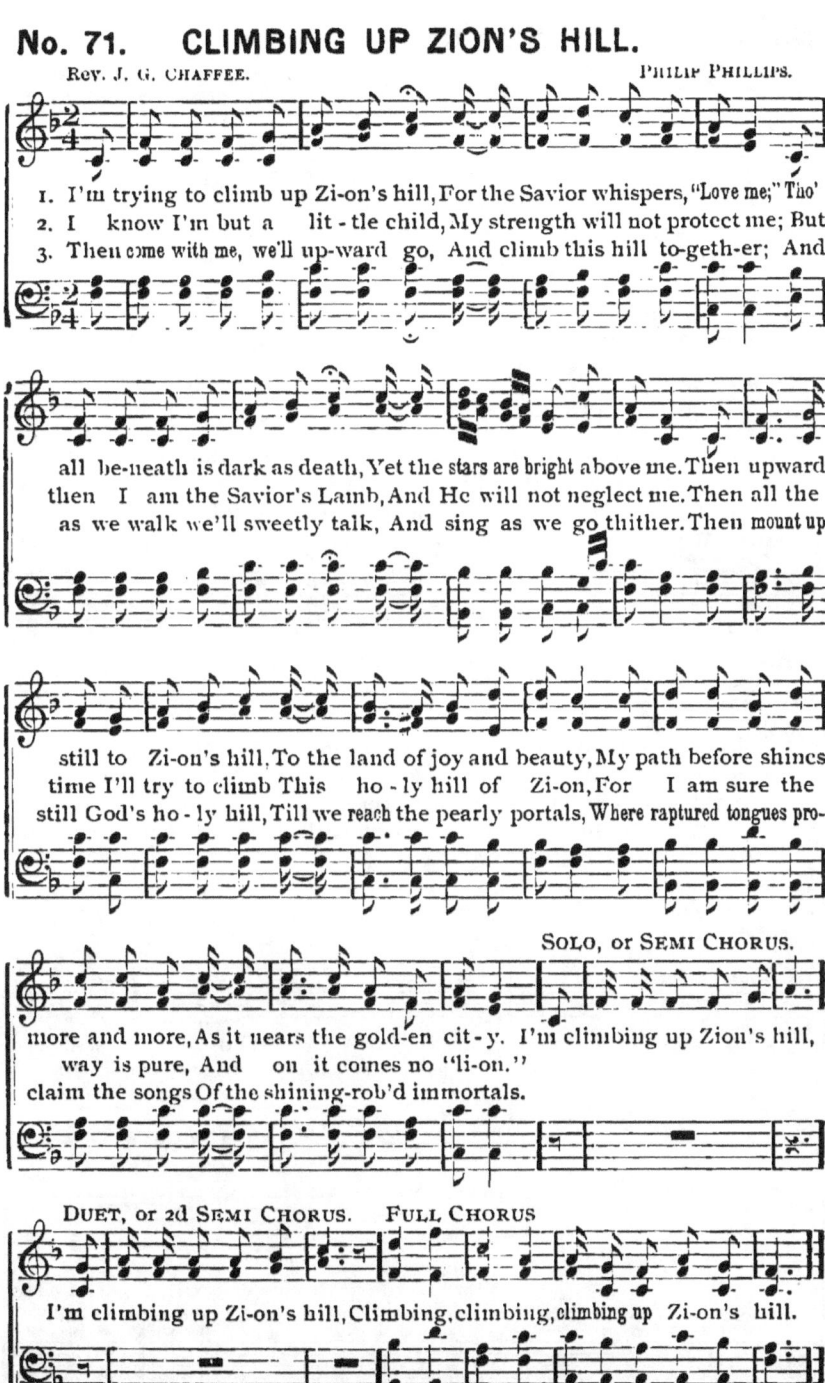

Come to the Crimson Fountain.

Come . . . . to the crimson fount - - ain, And
Come to the crim-son fount - ain, Wash thy sins a - way,
wash thy sins a - - way. . . . .
Come to the fount-ain, and wash thy sins a - way. . . . . .

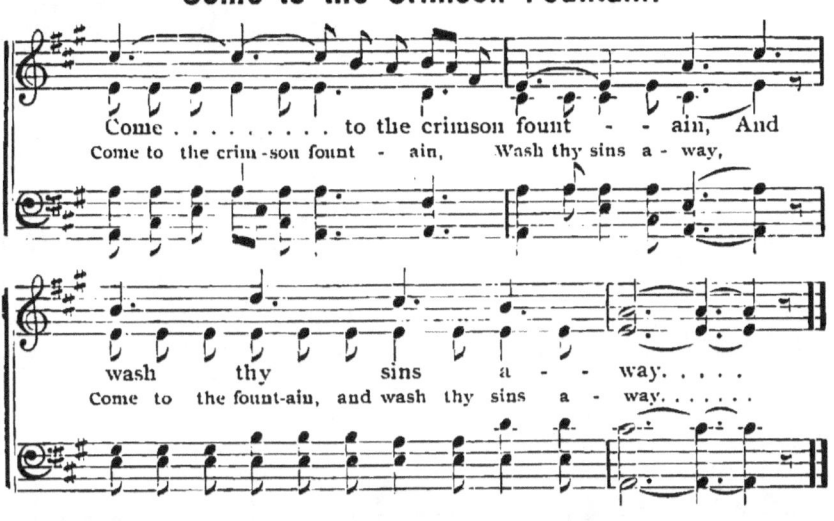

No. 77. THE CLEANSING WAVE.

MRS. PHŒBE PALMER. MRS. JOS. F. KNAPP.

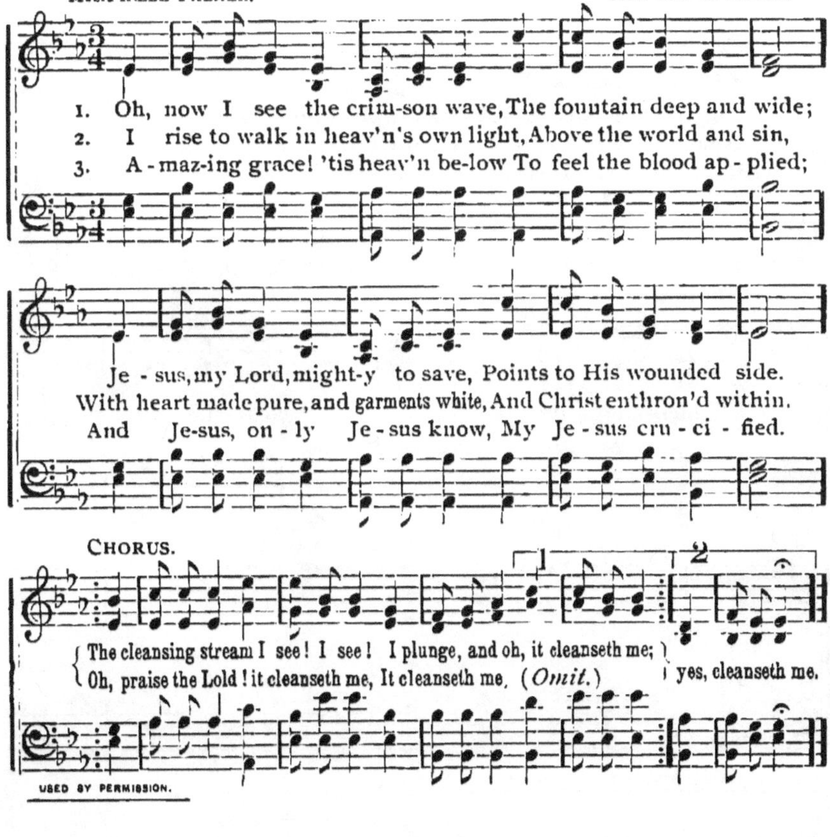
1. Oh, now I see the crim-son wave, The fountain deep and wide;
2. I rise to walk in heav'n's own light, Above the world and sin,
3. A-maz-ing grace! 'tis heav'n be-low To feel the blood ap-plied;
Je - sus, my Lord, might-y to save, Points to His wounded side.
With heart made pure, and garments white, And Christ enthron'd within.
And Je-sus, on - ly Je - sus know, My Je - sus cru - ci - fied.
CHORUS.
1 2
The cleansing stream I see! I see! I plunge, and oh, it cleanseth me;
Oh, praise the Lold! it cleanseth me, It cleanseth me. (Omit.)
yes, cleanseth me.

USED BY PERMISSION.

No. 79. I'LL BEAR THE CROSS.

Mrs. Harriet E. Jones.   Rev. W. S. Nickle.

1. Al-tho' a storm-y road I tread, I'll trust in Je-sus all the way;
2. Al-tho' the clouds obscure my sky, And sorrow's waves around me rise,
3. Al-tho' the thorns now pierce my feet, A-long a rough and dreary road,

A home of rest is just a-head, Where I shall live with Him, some day.
With Him who whispers, "It is I," I'll dwell, some day, 'neath fair-er skies.
There is a rest and joy com-plete, In my Redeemer's bright abode.

CHORUS.

I'll journey on beneath the cross, Till Je-sus bids me lay it down;

I'll shout and sing 'mid pain and loss, Till called where waits my fadeless crown.

Copyright, 1894, by Chas. H. Gabriel.

No. 83. **THE MARANATHA CRY.**

Rev. J. M. Orrock.   Chas. H. Gabriel.

1. O there is much to make us sad in this dark world of ours! The serpent's
 trail is oft-en seen a-mong its fairest flow'rs.
 But we must nev-er yield to grief, or, fall-ing, hopeless lie: We'll fling our
 ban-ner to the [*Omit.* . . . . .] breeze, and "Maranatha" cry.

2. What tho' the hosts of hell are strong and bold in what they say, The Lord of
 hosts is on our side, we're sure to win the day!
 The Vic-tor of the cross and tomb is seated now on high; We'll fling our
 ban-ner to the [*Omit.* . . . . .] breeze, and "Maranatha" cry.

3. Out of this world of sinners lost, grace saves a countless throng; And earth it-
 self shall be renewed, redeemed from ev'ry wrong
 When, therefore, trials crowd our way, and foes the right defy, We'll fling our
 ban-ner to the [*Omit.* . . . . .] breeze, and "Maranatha" cry.

CHORUS.

Our Lord reigneth! glo-ry be un-to His name, Our Lord reigneth,
Our dear Lord reigneth!   Our dear Lord reigneth,
now and ev-er-more the same; Tho' friends forsake and foes assail, They
cannot o-ver us prevail; We'll fling our banner to the breeze, and "Maranatha" cry.

COPYRIGHT, 1894, BY CHAS. H. GABRIEL.

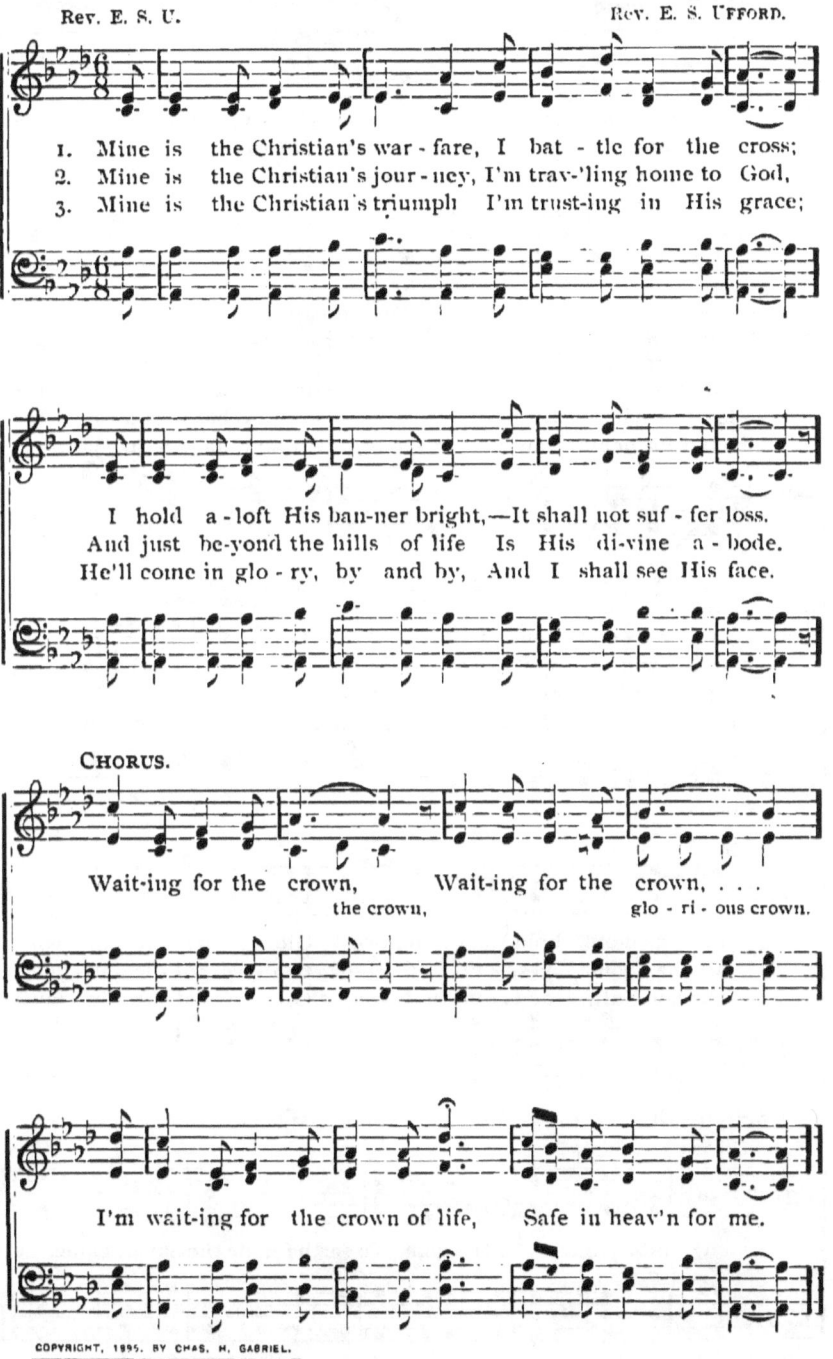

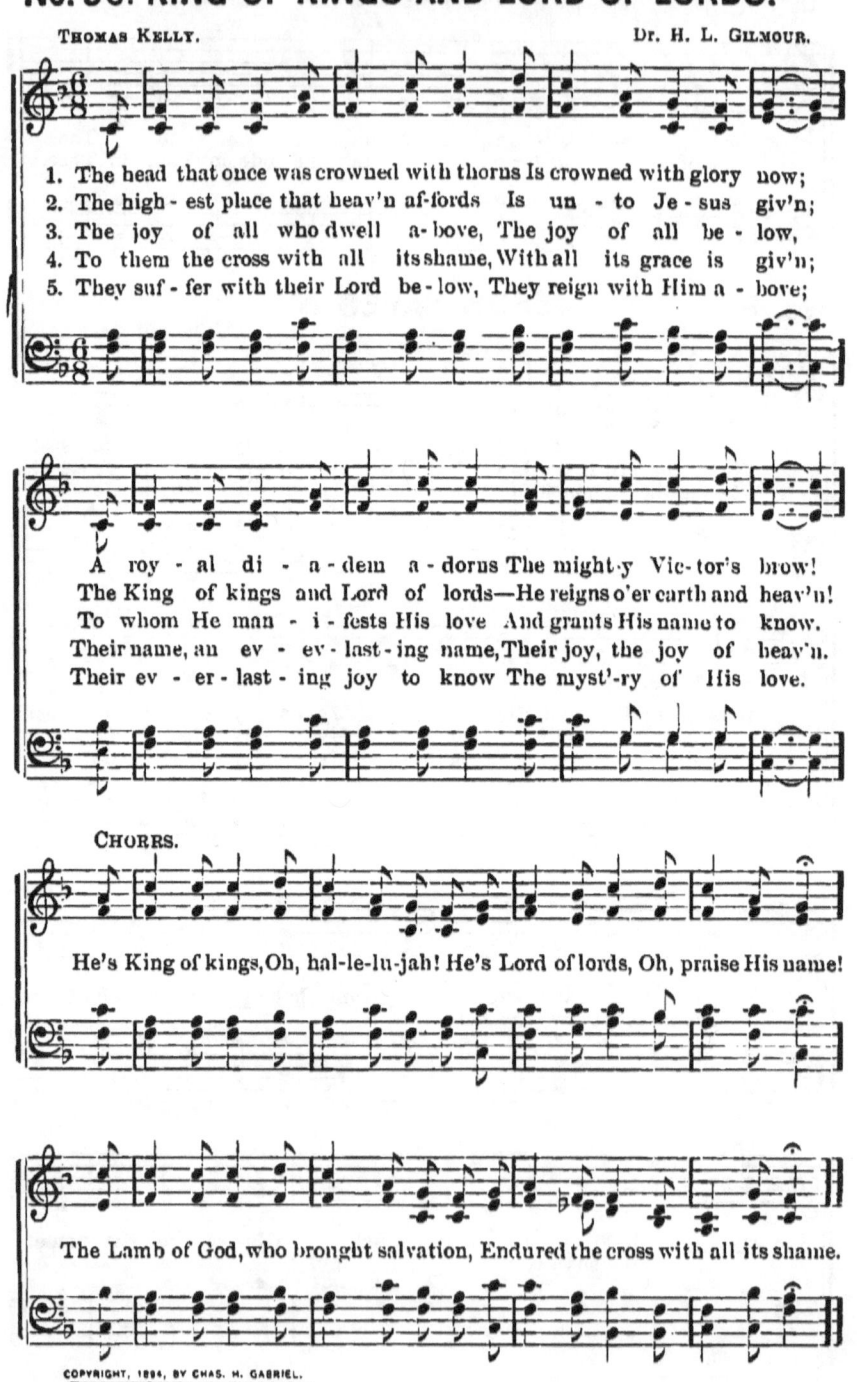

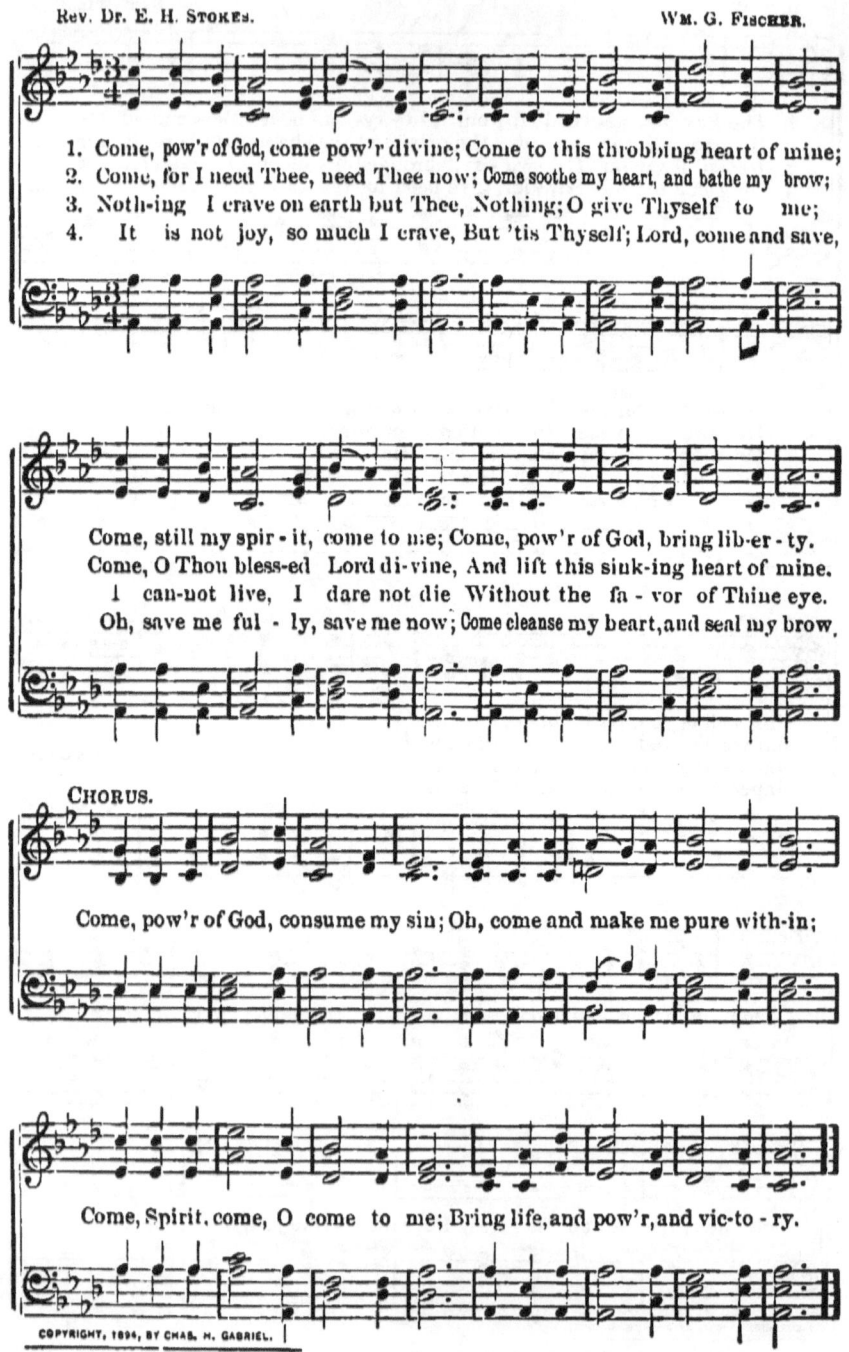

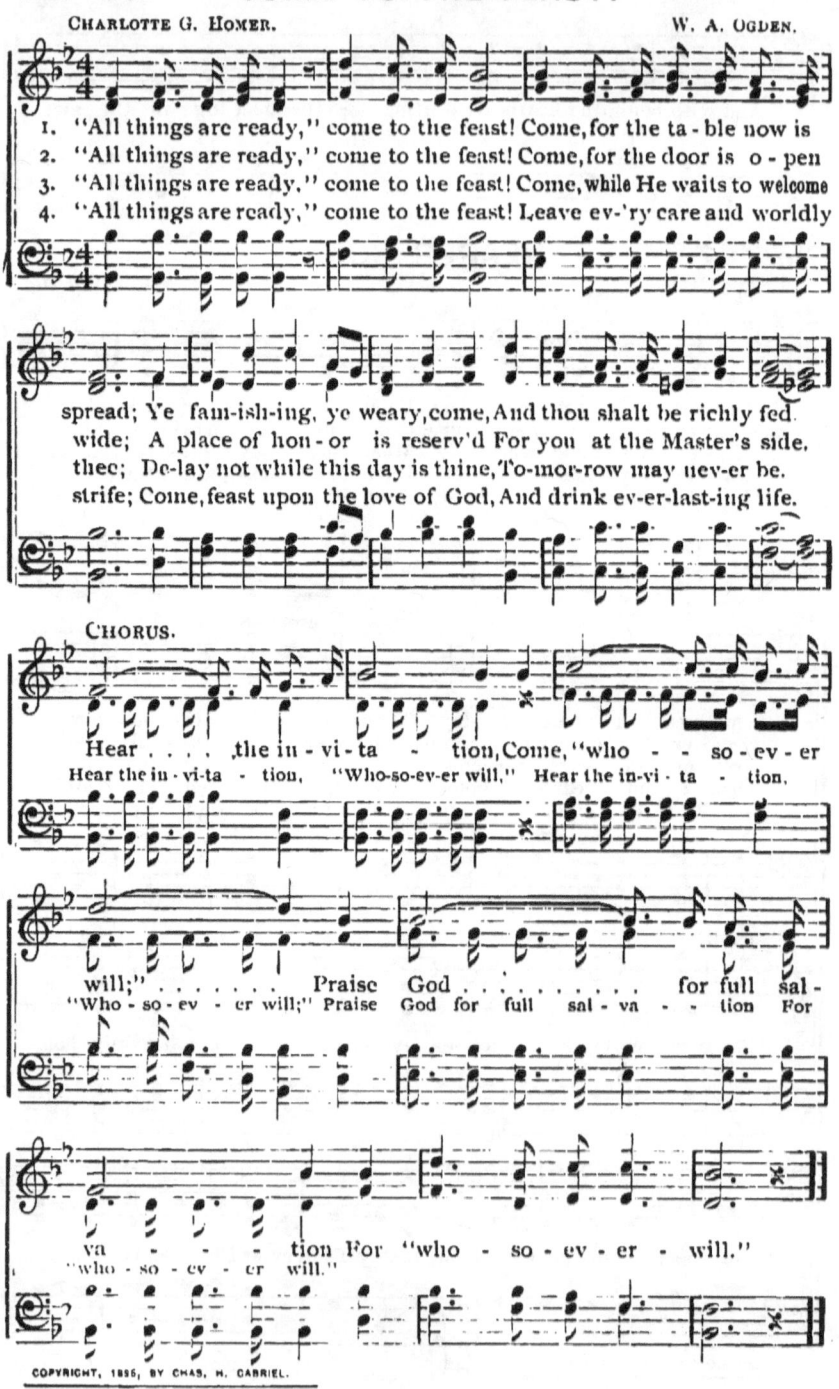

No. 111. ALL THE WORLD FOR JESUS.

GRACE WEISER DAVIS. J. H. FILLMORE.

1. All the world for Je - sus! Be this our ear - nest aim:
To spread the bless-ed ti - dings Of Him who once was slain.
2. All the world for Je - sus! Let each one pray and give,
Un - til re - mot-est na-tions Shall look to Him and live.
3. All the world for Je - sus! We'll give, at His be - hest,
To raise the poor and help-less, Till all have Christ confessed.
4. All the world for Je - sus! And Je - sus for the world!
For - ev - er be His ban - ner Of vic - to - ry un-furled.

CHORUS.

All the world for Je - sus, Let ev - 'ry crea-ture sing;
All the world for Je - sus, Our great e - ter - nal King.

COPYRIGHT, 1894, BY CHAS. H. GABRIEL.

No. 113. SING THE LOVE OF JESUS.

Mrs. HARRIET E. JONES.　　　　　　　　　　　　　CHAS. H. GABRIEL.

1. Sing, O sing the dear old sto-ry Of our Savior's matchless love;
2. Sing of love to you so precious, Tell, in song, how Jesus died;
3. Ye redeem'd ones, sing the story! Sing it o'er and o'er a-gain;

Sing of Je-sus and His glo-ry With the ransom'd host a-bove.
Let sweet mu-sic draw the millions To the dear Redeemer's side.
Un-till ev-'ry tribe and nation, Join to sing the glad re-frain.

CHORUS:

Sing, O sing . . . the love of Je - sus,— Sound His
Sing, O sing the love, the love of Je - sus,

prais - - es, far and near, . . Sing the won - drous sto-ry
Sound His prais-es, prais-es far and near, Sing the wondrous sto-ry

o - ver; 'Till the whole . . . wide world shall hear.
o - ver; 'Till the whole wide world shall hear.

COPYRIGHT, 1894, BY E. O. EXCELL. BY PER.

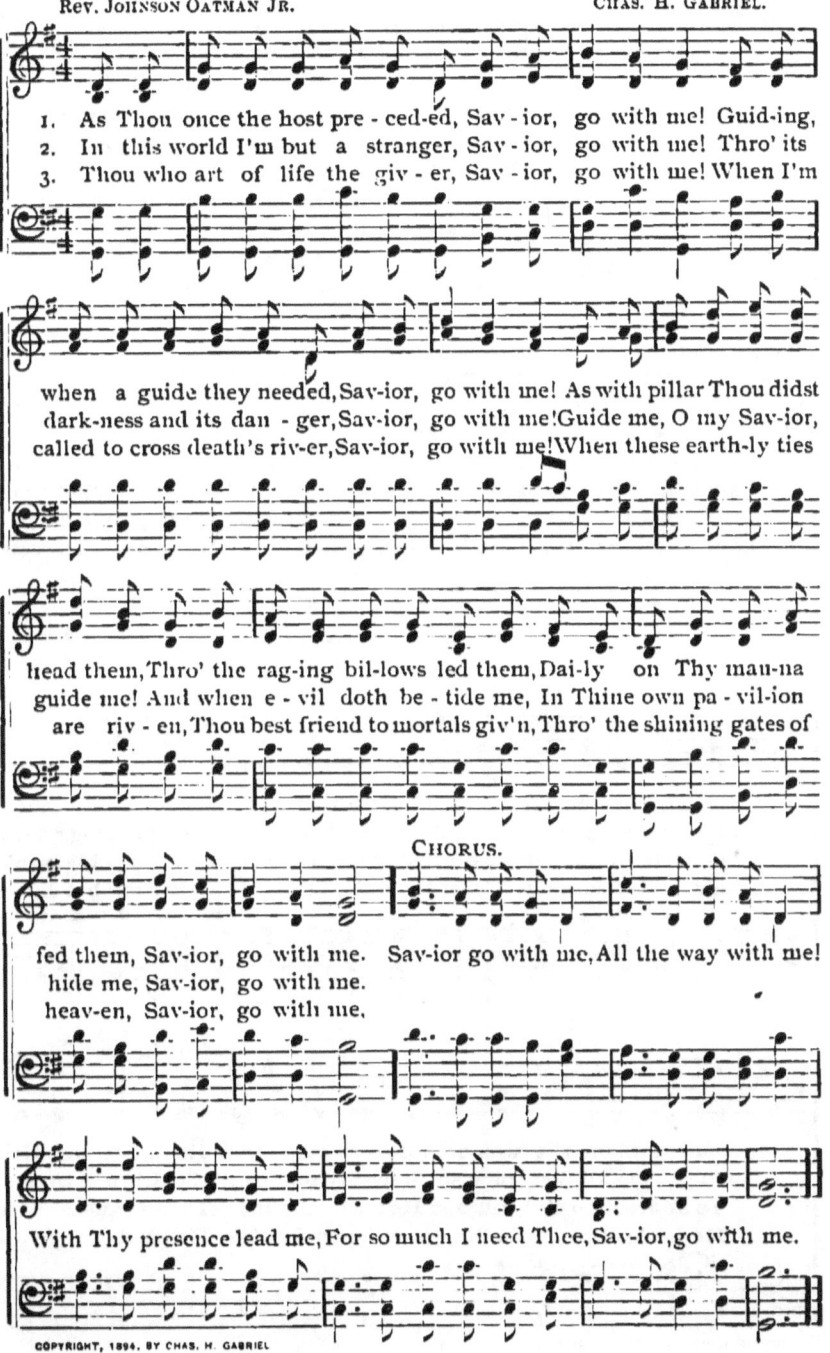

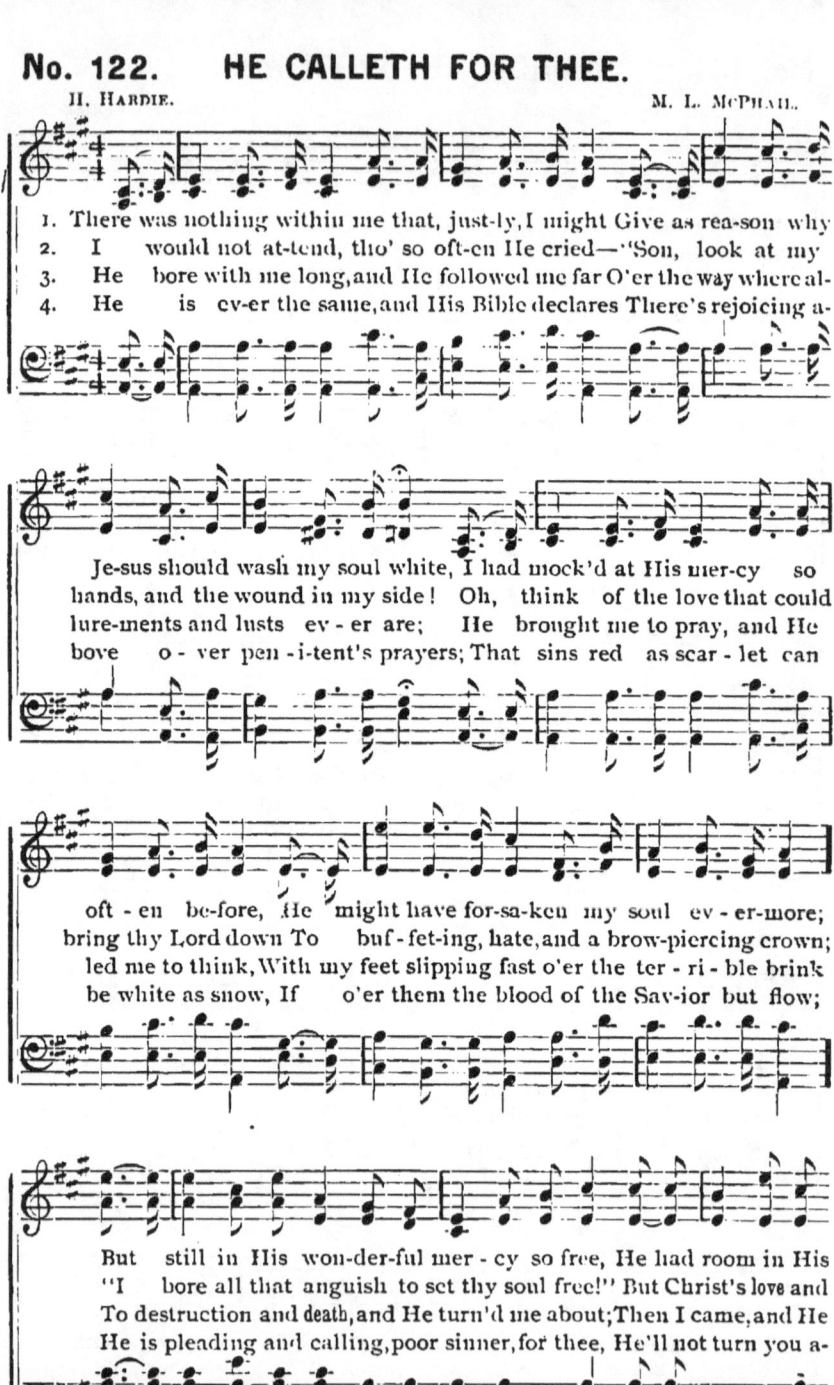

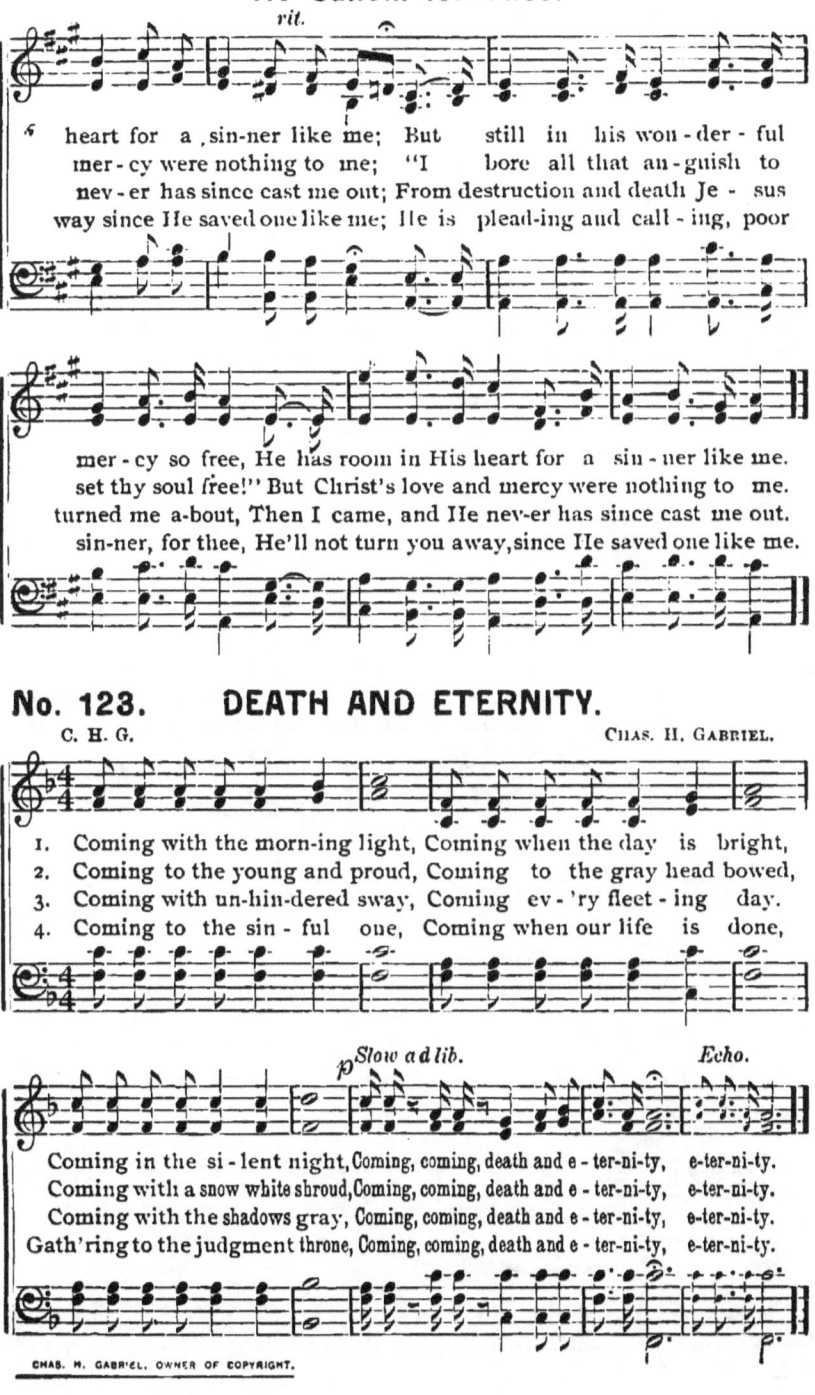

3 Nothing can for sin atone,
  Nothing but the blood of Jesus;
  Naught of good that I have done,
  Nothing but the blood of Jesus.

4 This is all my hope and peace—
  Nothing but the blood of Jesus;
  This is all my righteousness—
  Nothing but the blood of Jesus.

No. 138. NOT ASHAMED OF JESUS.

JOSEPH GRIGG.   CHAS. H. GABRIEL.

1. Je-sus, and shall it ever be, A mortal man ashamed of Thee?
2. Ashamed of Je-sus! sooner far Let ev'ning blush to own her star;
3. Ashamed of Je-sus! just as soon Let midnight be ashamed of noon;

Ashamed of Thee, whom angels praise, Whose glories shine thro' end-less days.
He sheds the beams of light di-vine O'er this be-night-ed soul of mine.
'Tis midnight with my soul till He, Bright morning Star, bids dark-ness flee.

CHORUS.

Ashamed of Je - sus I nev-er, I nev-er will be, ...
                                                           I nev-er will be,

For my dear Sav - ior is not ashamed of me; . . . . . . No! when I
                                      is not ashamed of me;

blush . . . be this my shame, That I no more re-vere His name.
                                    That I no more revere His name.

COPYRIGHT, 1894, BY CHAS. H. GABRIEL.

No. 141. SOMETIME, BY AND BY.

CHARLOTTE G. HOMER. Rev. L. H. BAKER.

1. I heard the reap-ers' hap-py song, When toils of day were o'er,
2. In fan-cy I have heard the song The ran-somed sweetly sing,
3. No more, O Lord, will I re-pine, No more im-pa-tient be;

As, troop-ing home-ward, one by one, Their gold-en sheaves they bore;
And longed to join my voice with theirs, In prais-es to the King;
But, with a will-ing heart and mind, I'll bear the cross for Thee!

And, as I pray'd their joys to share, There came this sweet re-ply:
"Be pa-tient," spake the voice a-gain, "The mo-ment draw-eth nigh!
Then, when my name is called in heav'n, On wings of love I'll fly!

rit. ad lib. FINE.

"Toil on! thou, too, shalt come with joy, Some-time, by and by."
Thou, too, shalt sing around my throne, Some-time, by and by!"
For well I know that day will come, Some-time, by and by.
Some-time, by and by.

REFRAIN. D.S

Some-time, some-time, Some-time, yes, by and by!
Some-time, by and by,

COPYRIGHT, 1895, BY CHAS. H. GABRIEL.

Pardoned, Cleansed, Redeemed.

Pardoned, cleansed, redeemed am I, While I live, or should I die.

No. 143. ALL THINE OWN.

MAGGIE E. GREGORY. GEO. H. CROSBY.

1. Sav-ior, our hearts shall be Thy throne, Our love shall be Thy crown;
2. Not as the cru-el crown of thorns, In Pilate's judg-ment hall;
3. Sav-ior, our hearts shall by Thy throne, Our lives shall be Thy praise,-
4. Ac-cept our hum-ble of-fer-ing, Come, reign up-on Thy throne;

And at Thy sa-cred, pierc-ed feet, Our off'rings lay we down.
Thy crown to-day shall be our love, Our tal-ents, and our all.
And for Thy glo-ry we will live, Thro' all our fut-ure days.
Our lives, our souls, our all we bring; Lord, seal us Thine a-lone.

CHORUS.

All Thine own, Thine a-lone Sav-ior, our love shall be Thy crown;

All Thine own, Thine a-lone, Our hearts shall be Thy throne.

No. 146. SEVEN TIMES 'ROUND.

ADA BLENKHORN.   H. A. H.

1. While you on-ward fare, in the nar-row way To the heav'n that lies be-fore you; The cit-y of doubt on your path may rise, With its shad-ows rest-ing o'er you.
2. There are foes to fight, there are wrongs to right, Ere the cit-y fade be-fore you; 'Gainst the hosts of sin you will sure-ly win. For your Cap-tain fight-eth for you.
3. With the Spir-it's sword, and the shield of faith, Ad-vance! your Lord com-mand-eth; For the ban-ner white of His ho-ly cross, Must wave where the cit-y stand-eth.

CHORUS.

Seven times 'round, go seven times 'round, When the cit-y of Doubt is be-fore you! With the song of hope, and the pray'r of faith! And its walls will fall be-fore you.

COPYRIGHT, 1895, BY CHAS. H. GABRIEL.

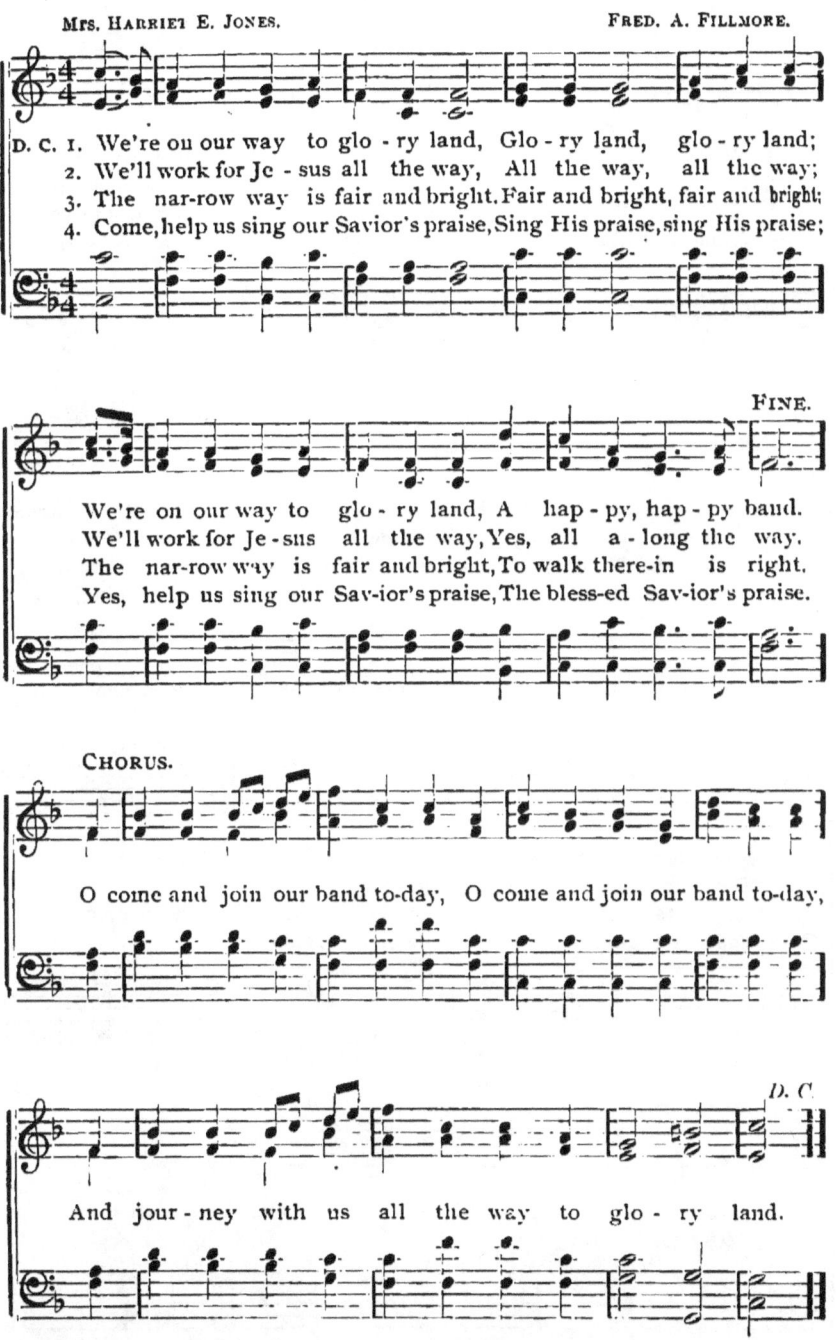

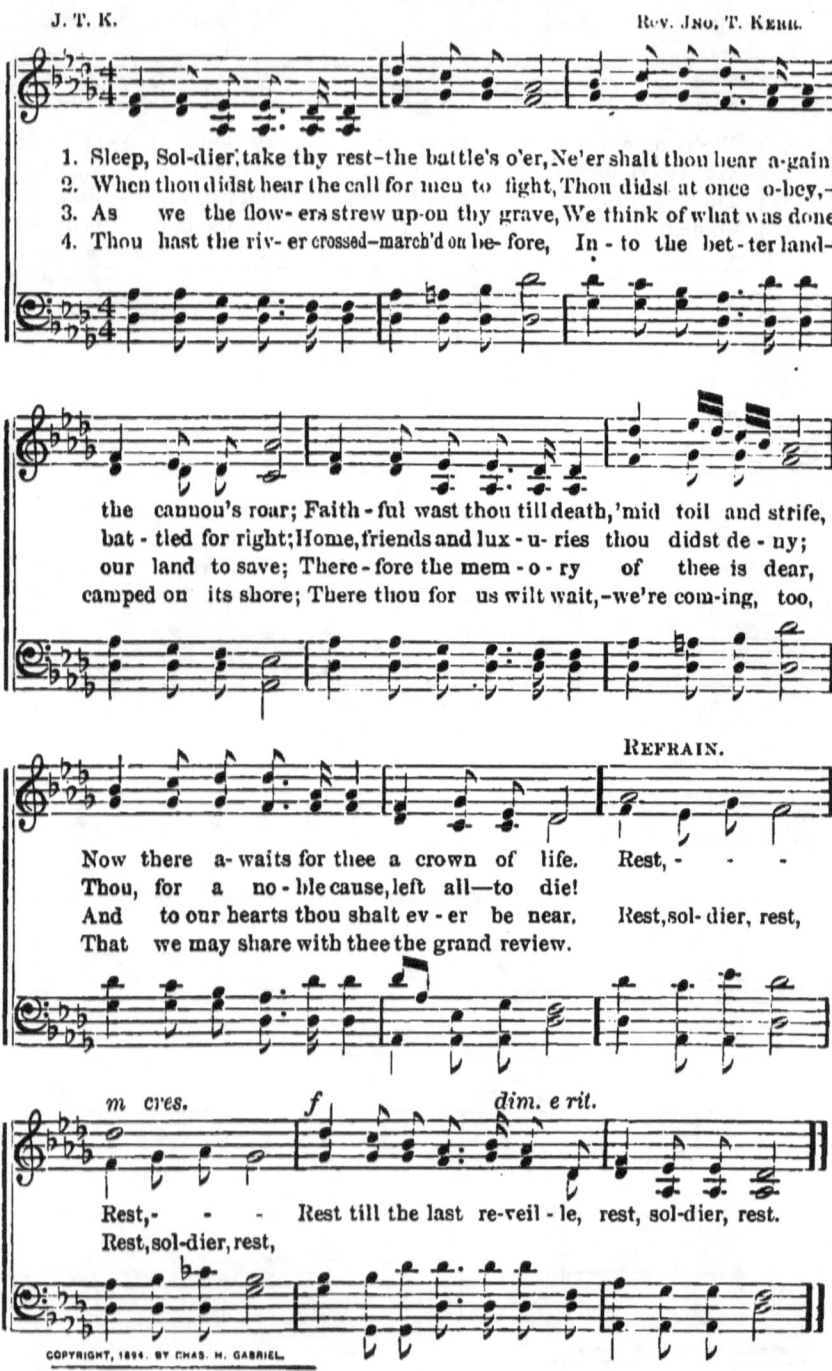

God is Good.

No. 155. DRAW ME NEARER.

Mrs. L. M. Beal Bateman.   Fred. A. Fillmore.

1. I want my heart made pur-er, Lord, More sanc-ti-fied by Thee,
2. I know my earth-ly sight is dim, But Thou the blind can'st heal,
3. So cleanse me by thy wondrous grace, From sin so set me free,

Till thro' the mist-y doubts of earth, Thy glo-ry I may see.
And clear-ly to my long-ing soul, Thy-self Thou can'st re-veal.
That I in all His ho-li-ness My bless-ed Lord may see.

CHORUS.

So draw me near-er, near-er, Make my path-way clear-er;

Oh, draw me near-er, near-er, My bless-ed Lord to Thee.

COPYRIGHT, 1891, BY FILLMORE BROS.

No. 156. THERE'S ROOM ON BOARD.

The stanzas should be sung by two separate quartetts, singing alternately the questions and answers. All unite on the chorus.

ADA BLENKHORN.   H. A. HENRY.

1. Ho, sail-ors on the Christian's sea, Is there a place on board for me?
2. Ho, sail-ors! whom have you on board, Your Guide and safe-ty to af-ford?
3. Ho, sail-or! whither bound are ye Up-on this calm, untroubled sea?

By angry waves my boat is toss'd, I fear, I fear I shall be lost!
Christ is our Pi-lot true, and He Will bring us safe-ly o'er the sea.
To glo-ry port our way we take, The harbor with our Lord we'll make.

CHORUS.

Yes, brother, yes! there's room, there's room on board, The in-vi-ta-tion's from our Lord; Your fare is paid! . . . . . the way is
your fare is paid,

free, . - . . . . . Come, sail with us the Chris-tian's sea.
the way is free,

COPYRIGHT, 1895, BY CHAS. H. GABRIEL.

As a Shepherd.

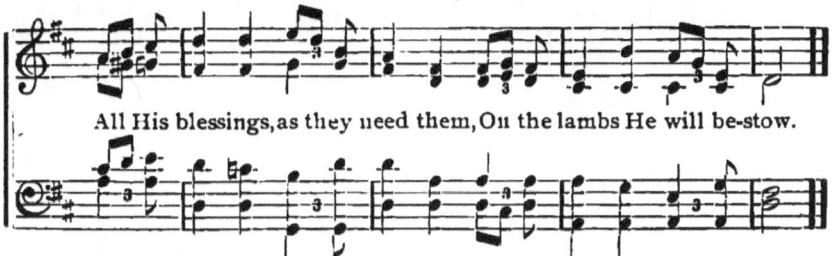

All His blessings, as they need them, On the lambs He will bestow.

No. 161.　　I AM THE DOOR,

Rev. Dwight Williams, by per.　　　　Arr. by C. H. G.

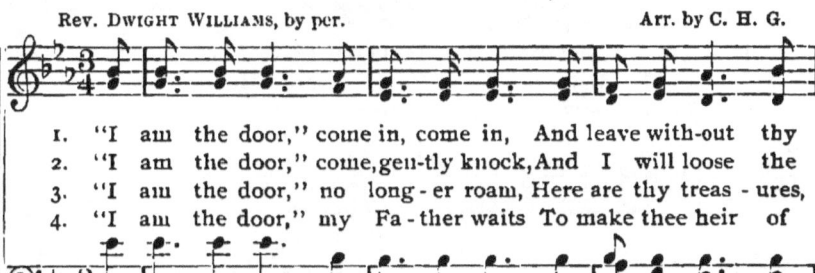

1. "I am the door," come in, come in, And leave without thy
2. "I am the door," come, gently knock, And I will loose the
3. "I am the door," no longer roam, Here are thy treasures,
4. "I am the door," my Father waits To make thee heir of

load of sin; The night is dark, the storm is wild, Oh,
heav-y lock, That guards my Father's precious fold; Come
here thy home; I pur-chased them for thee and thine, And
rich es-tates; Come, dwell with Him and dwell with me, And

venture in, thou stranger child, Oh, venture in, thou stranger child.
in from darkness and from cold, Come in from darknes and from cold.
paid the price in blood divine, And paid the price in blood divine.
thou my Father's child shall be, And thou my Father's child shall be.

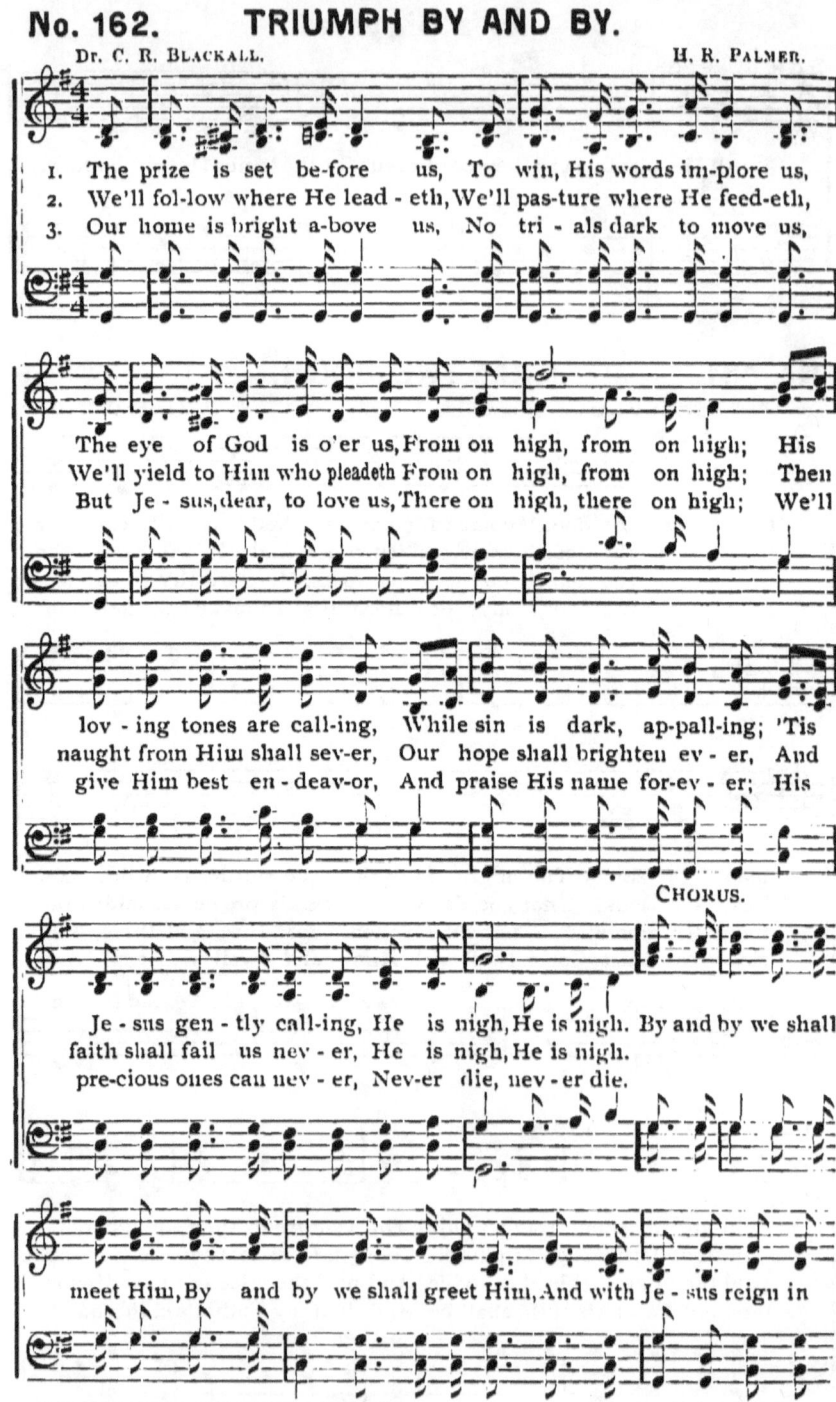

Triumph By and By.

glo-ry, By and by, by and by; By and by we shall meet Him, By and by we shall greet Him, And with Je-sus reign in glo-ry, By and by;

No. 163. CONSECRATION.

Mrs. MARY D. JAMES.   Mrs. JOS. F. KNAPP.

1. My bod-y, soul, and spir-it, Je-sus, I give to Thee, A conse-crated oft'ring, Thine ev-er-more to be.
2. O Je-sus, might-y Sav-ior, I trust in Thy great name, I look for Thy sal-va-tion, Thy promise now I claim.
3. Oh, let the fire de-scend-ing Just now up-on my soul, Consume my hum-ble oft'ring, And cleanse and make me whole.
4. I'm Thine, O precious Jesus, Wash'd by Thy pre-cious blood; Now seal me by Thy Spir-it, A sac-ri-fice to God.

REFRAIN.

My all is on the al-tar, I'm wait-ing for the fire; Waiting, waiting, waiting, I'm wait-ing for the fire.

Rit.

BY PERMISSION.

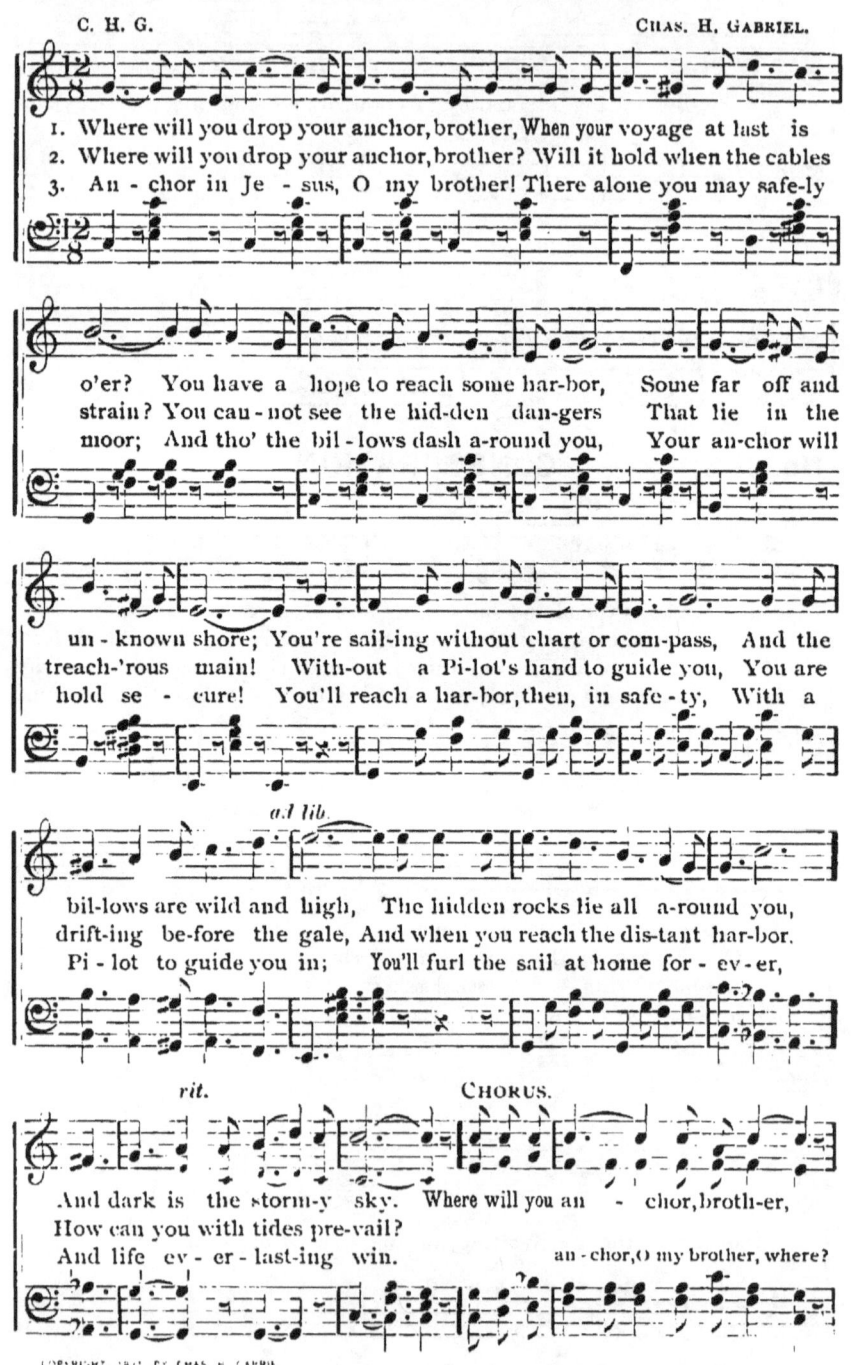

Where Will You Anchor?

Where will you an-chor?   Where?......
Oh, where   Where will you an - chor? Where will you an - chor?

No. 165 SHOUT THE TIDINGS.

D. M. C.   D. M. Chute.

1. Shout the ti-dings of sal - va-tion. Bear the mes-sage far and wide;
2. Shout the ti-dings of sal - va-tion, Sit not i - dly by the way;
3. Shout the ti-dings of sal - va-tion, Spread the word from shore to shore!

Spread the feast for ev - 'ry na-tion—Tell of Je - sus cru - ci - fied!
Heed the message of the Mas-ter:—"Go and work for me to-day."
Je - sus' mer - cy is un-measured, And His love a boundless store!

CHORUS.

Hal - le - lu - jah for Je - sus! Shout the ti - dings a - gain!

Hal - le - lu - jah for Je - sus, Now and ev - er! A - men.

COPYRIGHT, 1893, BY CHAS. H. GABRIEL.

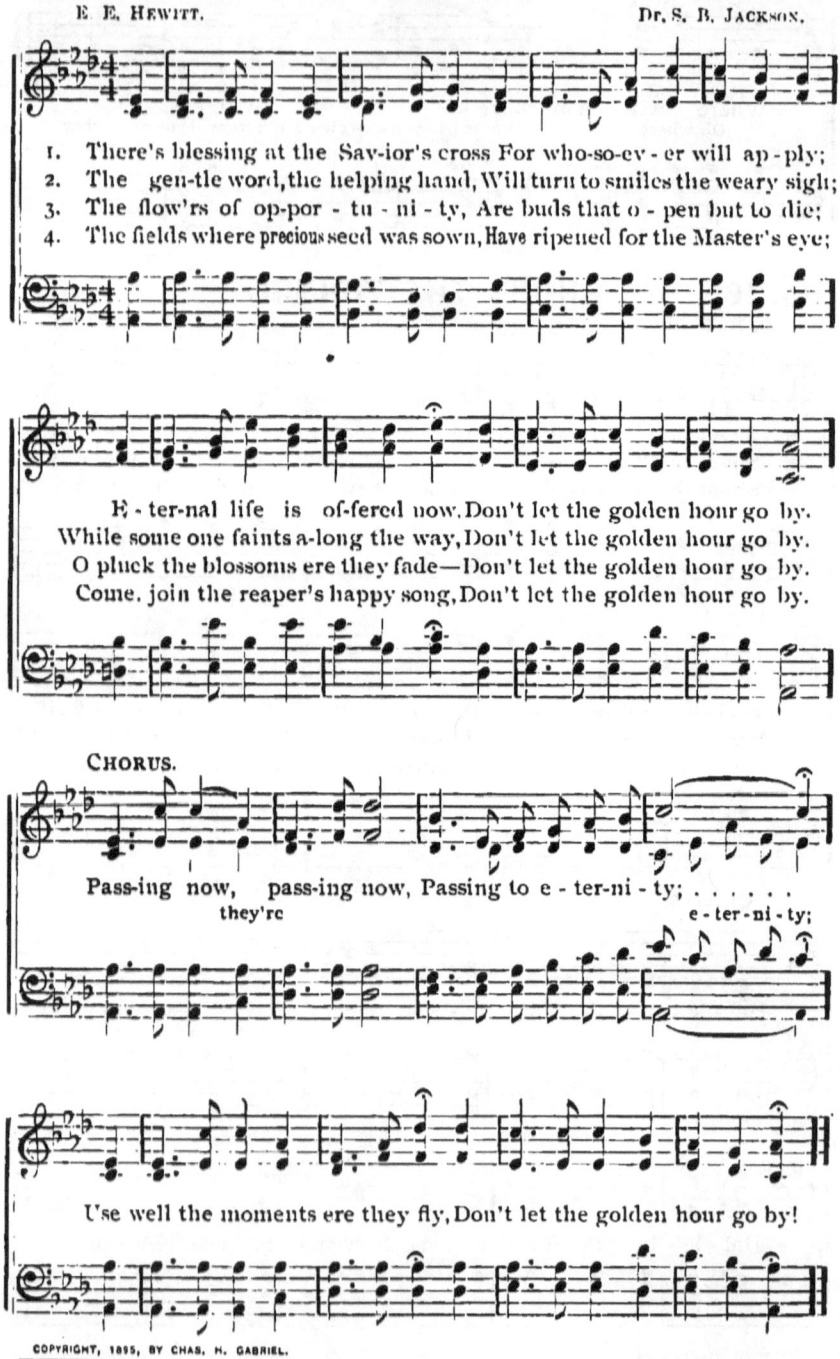

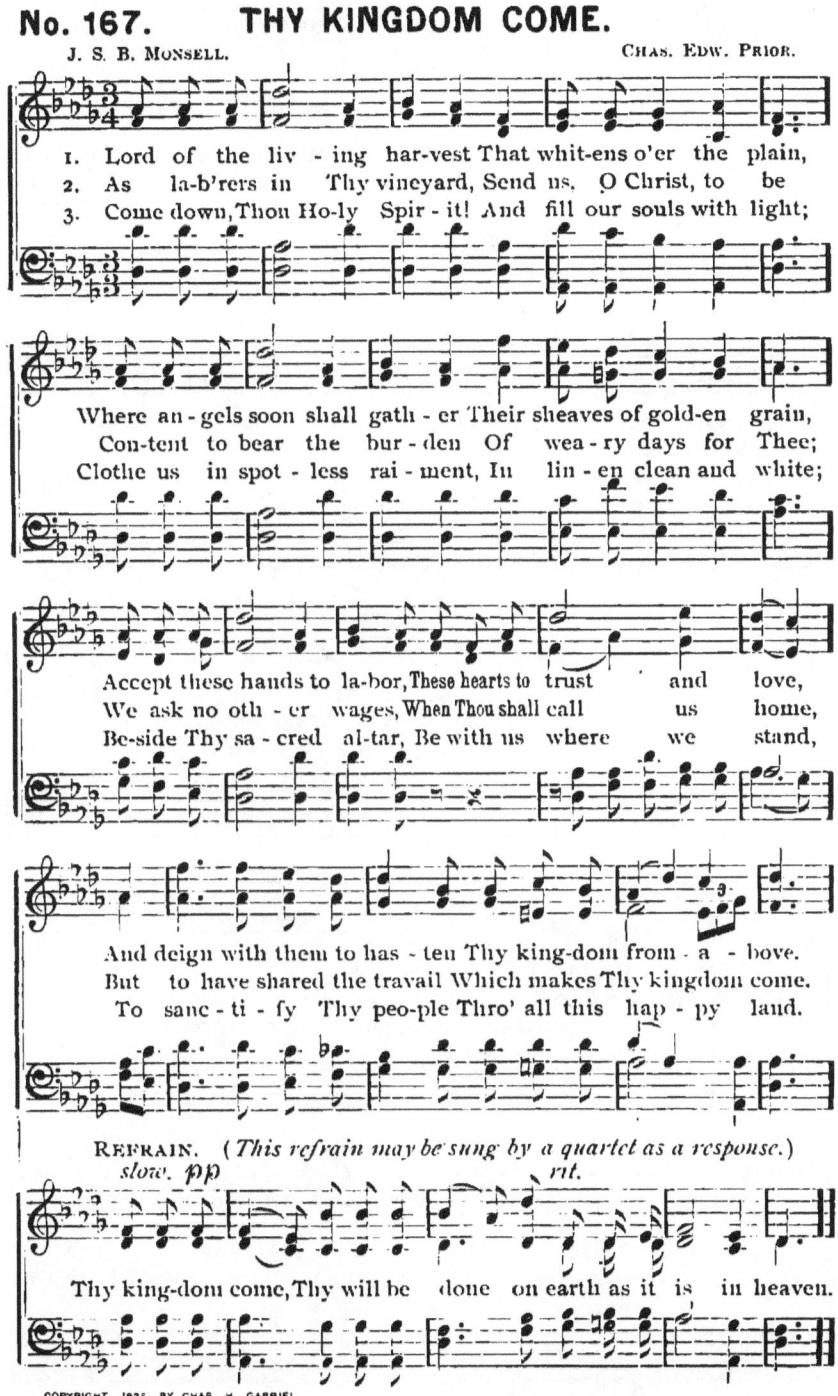

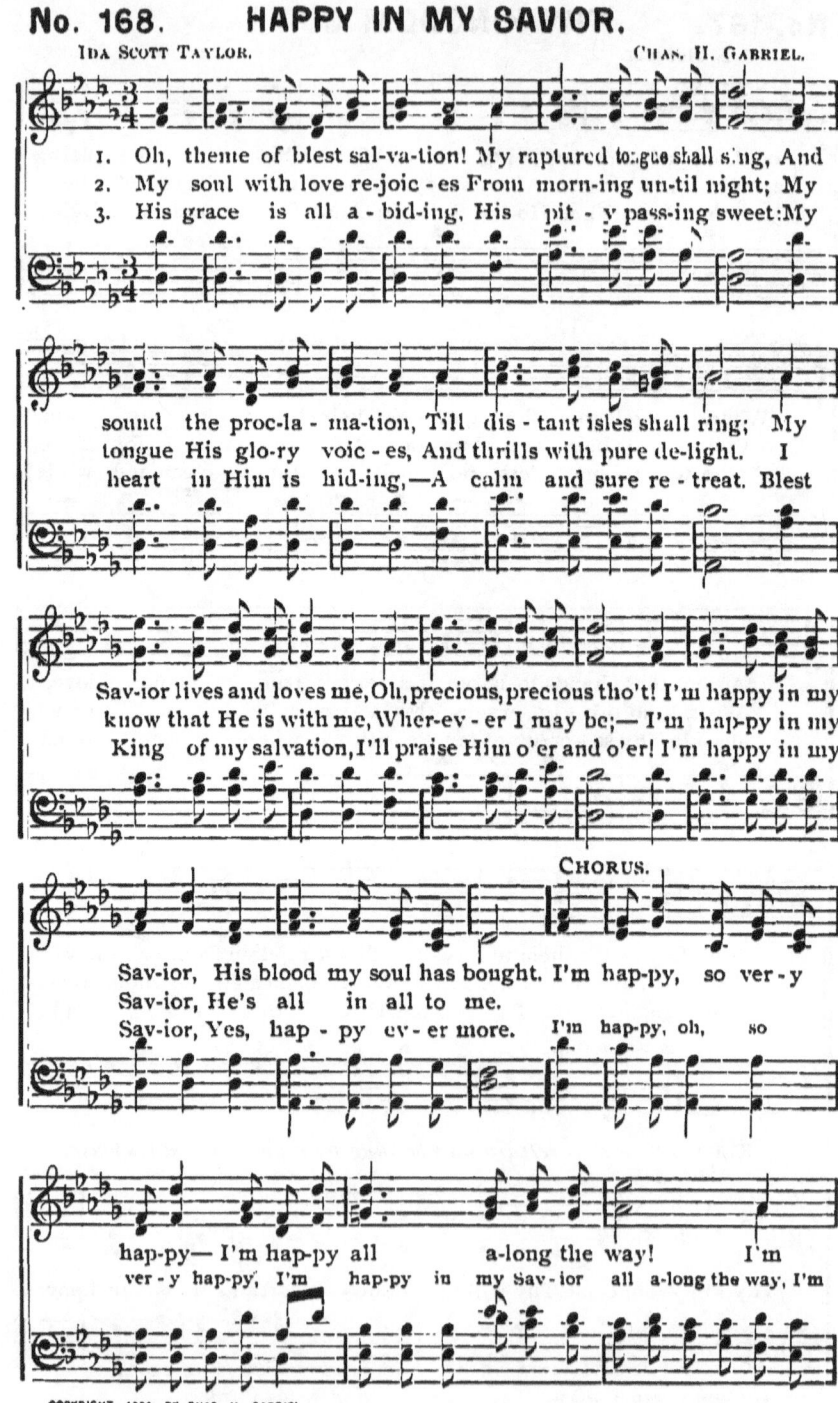

Happy in My Savior.

hap-py, so ver-y hap-py in Je - sus all the day!
hap-py, oh, so ver-y hap-py in Je-sus, hap-py all the day!

No. 169. LIVING FOR CHRIST.

ADALINE H. BEERY.   A. S. DE YOE.

1. We come to Thee, O ho-ly Christ, To learn Thy gracious ways,
2. Let ev-'ry treas-ure yield to Thee, Thou Rose of Sharon sweet;
3. O fill us with a ho-ly zeal, To make Thy graces known,

And frame our con-duct and de-sires, To Thy sin-cer-est praise.
And for Thy pure com-pan-ion-ship, O make our spir-its meet.
That all the world may glad-ly come, And kneel before Thy throne.

CHORUS.

Liv-ing for Christ! O joy supreme! Our ev-er-last-ing Friend;
our Friend;
We con-se-crate our all to Thee, 'Till life and tho't shall end.

COPYRIGHT, 1894, BY CHAS. H. GABRIEL.

No. 172. **WILL YOU GO?**

FRED. WOODROW.   J. H. TENNEY.

1. There is a land beyond the sea, Will you go? will you go?
2. No seasons come and pass away, Will you go? will you go?
3. Oh, still a-jar the pearly gate, Will you go? will you go?
                                            Will you go? will you go?

Where sin or pain can nev-er be, Will you go? will you go?
No night, but one e-ter-nal day, Will you go? will you go?
For you and me the angels wait, Will you go? will you go?
                                            Will you go? will you go?

Where those who weep, shall weep no more; Where storms of life and death are o'er,
There hun-ger, cold, distress and pain, Are seen no more, nor known a-gain;
Come! all who will may en-ter in; Yes, all a crown of life may win,

For-got-ten on that shining shore, Will you go? will you go?
There angels walk the shining plain, Will you go? will you go?
The soul be saved from death and sin, Will you go? will you go?
                                            Will you go? will you go?

COPYRIGHT 1893, BY CHAS. H. GABRIEL.

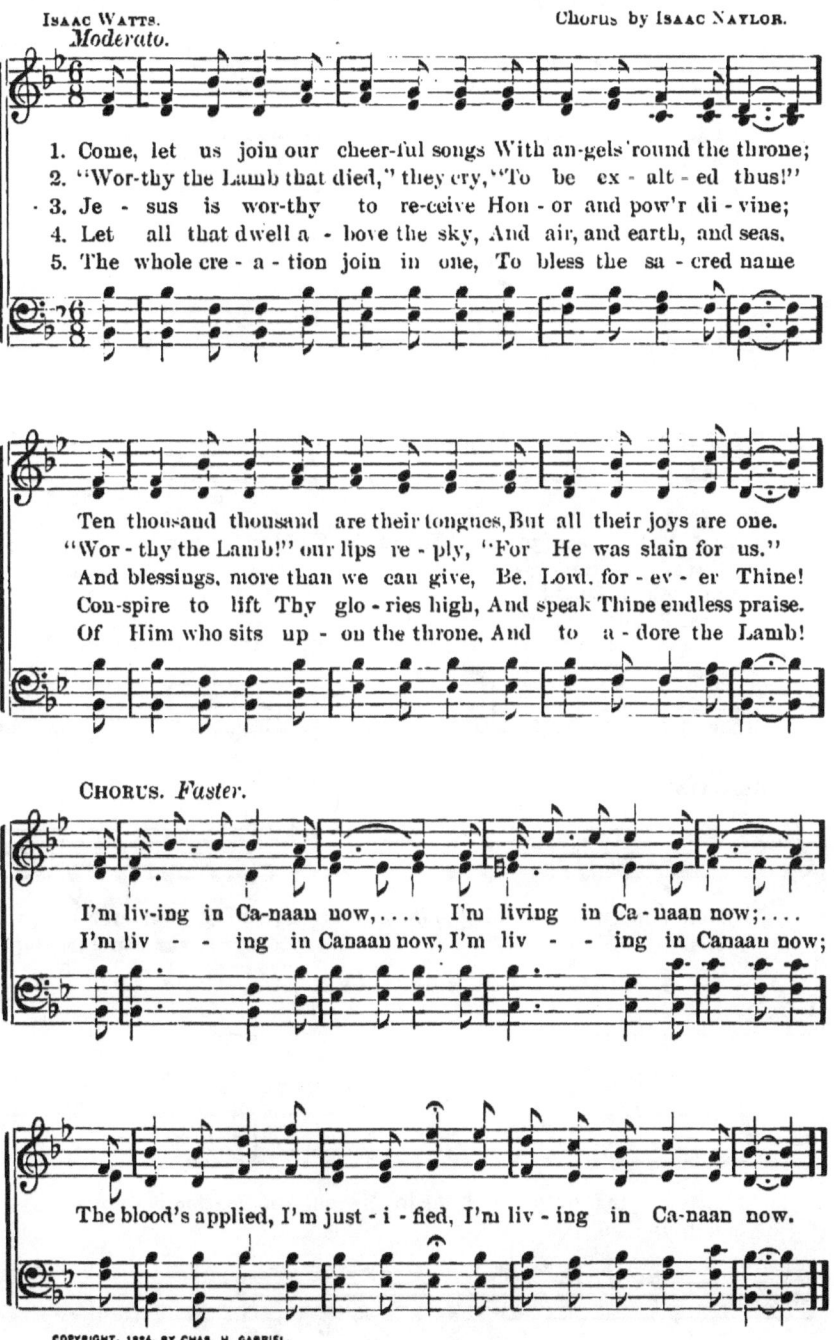

No. 174.   MARCHING TO ZION.

1. { Am I a sol-dier of the cross, Hal-low'd cross, bless-ed cross,
     And shall I fear to own His cause. Here be-low, here be-low,
2. { Must I be car-ried to the skies, Car-ried on, car-ried on,
     While oth-ers fought to win the prize Of His love, wondrous love,
3. { Sure I must fight if I would reign Ev-er-more, ev-er-more,
     I'll bear the cross, en-dure the pain All the way, all the way,

Am I a sol-dier of the cross, A fol-low'r of the Lamb? }
And shall I fear to own His cause, Or blush to speak His name? }
Must I be car-ried to the skies On flow-'ry beds of ease, }
While oth-ers fought to win the prize And sailed thro' bloody seas? }
Sure I must fight if I would reign: In-crease my cour-age Lord! }
I'll bear the cross, en-dure the pain, Sup-port-ed by Thy word. }

REFRAIN.

March - ing, we're marching to Zi-on, we're march-ing, yes, march-ing;
March-ing on,   march-ing on, yes, marching on;

March - ing, we're march-ing to Zi-on, And Je-sus is our song.
March-ing on,

COPYRIGHT, 1891, BY CHAS. H. GABRIEL.

Glory to the Lamb.

In the seat of pow'r enthrone Him, Crown the Savior King of Kings!

No. 179. THE SOUL'S REFUGE.

ANNE STEELE.   S. W. STRAUB.

1. Thou ref-uge of my soul, On Thee, when sor-rows rise, On Thee, when waves of troub-le roll, My faint-ing hope re-lies.
2. To Thee I tell my grief, For Thou a-lone canst heal; Thy word can bring a sweet re-lief For ev-'ry pain I feel.
3. But oh, when doubts pre-vail, I fear to call Thee mine; The spring of com-fort seems to fail, And all my hopes de-cline.
4. Yet, Lord, where shall I flee? Thou art my on-ly trust; And still my soul would cling to Thee, Tho' pros-trate in the dust.

CHORUS.

On Thee, on Thee, My hope re-lies,
On Thee, on Thee, My hope re-lies,
On Thee when waves of sor-row roll, My faint-ing hope re-lies.

COPYRIGHT, 1894, BY CHAS. H. GABRIEL.

No. 184. VALE OF BEULAH.

E. A. Hoffman. Joseph Garrison.

1. { I am pass-ing down the val-ley that they say is so lone,
     'Tis to me the vale of Beu-lah, 'tis a beau-ti-ful way,
2. { Not a sor-row, not a shad-ow ev-er dark-ens the way,
     And the mu-sic sweet-ly chant-ed by the heav-en-ly throng,
3. { So I jour-ney with re-joic-ing t'ward the Cit-y of Light,
     And I near the o-pen por-tals of the king-dom a-bove,

But I find that all the path-way is with flow'rs o-ver-grown. }
For the Sav-ior walks be-side me, my com-pan-ion each day. }
For a ra-diance bright as glo-ry shines up-on it all day; }
Floats in ca-dence down the val-ley, and it cheers me a-long. }
While each day my joy is deep-er, and the pathway more bright; }
For this high-way leads to Ca-naan, to the King-dom of love. }

CHORUS.

Vale of Beu-lah! Vale of Beu-lah! Thou art pre-cious to me;

For the love-ly land of Ca-naan In the dis-tance I see.

USED BY PER. OF E. A. HOFFMAN, OWNER OF COPYRIGHT.

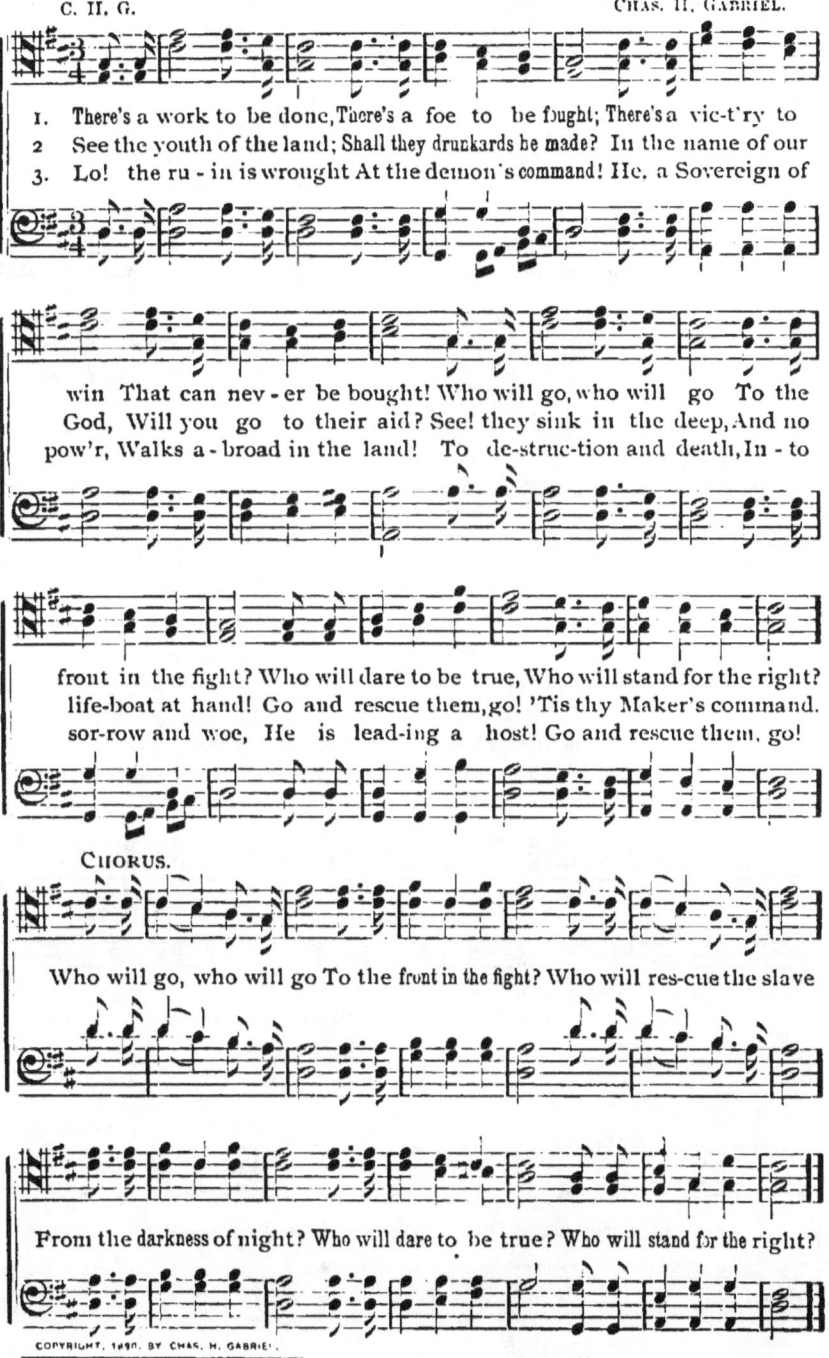

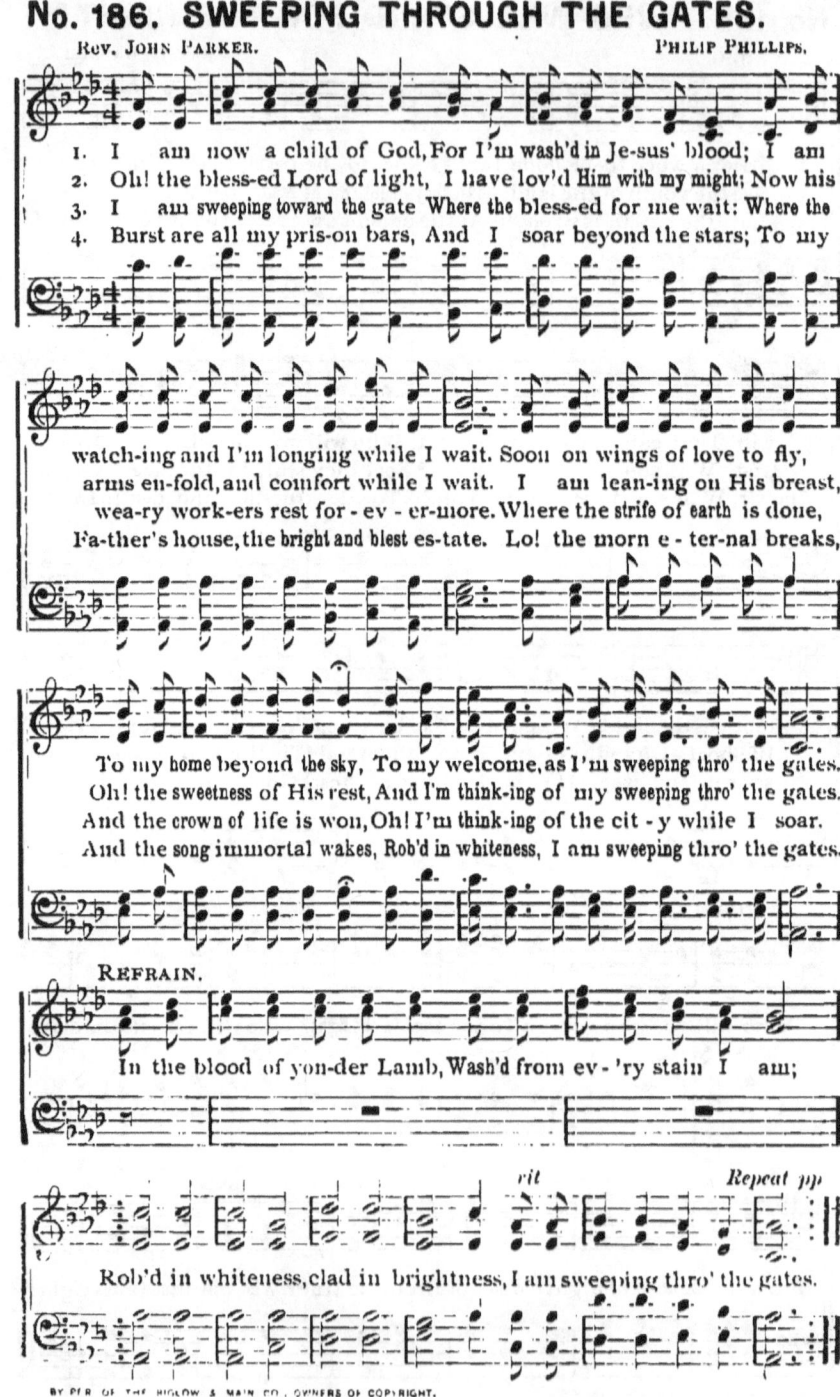

No. 188. YON PORTALS FAIR.

Rev. E. A. Hoffman. R. M. McIntosh.

1. When shall we stand at yon por-tals fair? By and by, by and by;
2. When will the la-bor of earth be o'er? By and by, by and by;
3. When will we see all our friends a-gain? By and by, by and by;
4. We have a prom-ise of bless-ed rest, By and by, by and by;

When shall we share in the glo-ry there? By and by, yes by and by.
When will we sor-row and sigh no more? By and by, yes by and by.
When shall we join them in sweet re-frain? By and by, yes by and by.
Lean-ing in calm-ness on Je-sus' breast, By and by, yes by and by.

'Twill not be long till the Lord shall come, Call me to en-ter my heav'nly home;
Not long on earth can the pilgrim stay; Soon God will summon to heav'n a-way;
'Twill not be long till in joy we meet, And in af-fec-tion each oth-er greet;
Not here where weary the heart and hand, But in the fairer Im-man-uel's land;

There with the ho-ly and blest to roam, By and by, yes, by and by.
Oh! it is com-ing, that glad, glad day, By and by, yes, by and by.
Oh! the re-un-ion will be so sweet, By and by, yes, by and by.
Crown'd with the host of the white-rob'd band, By and by, yes, by and by.

No. 192.   SCATTER SEED.

X. X. X.   J. L. MOORE.

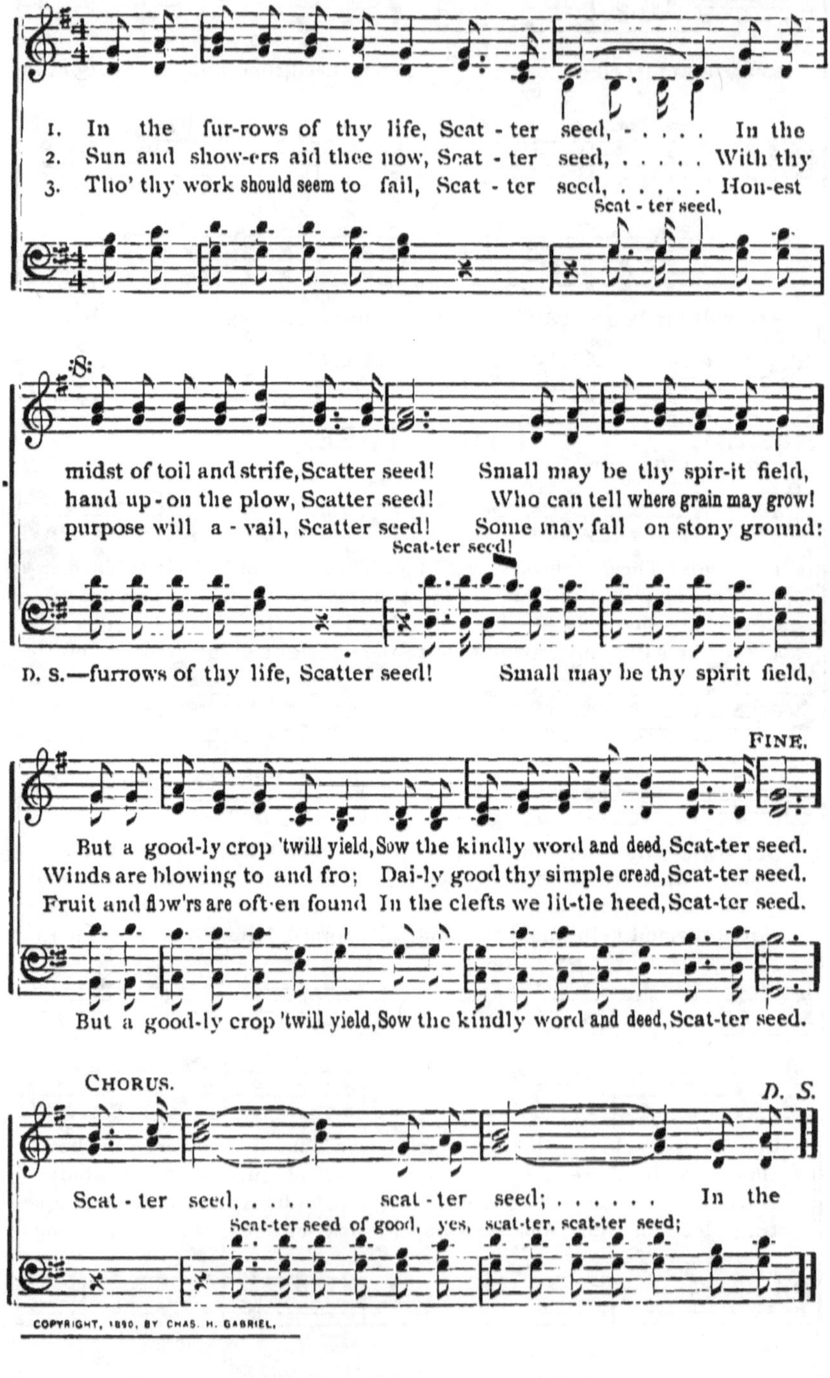

1. In the fur-rows of thy life, Scat-ter seed, ... In the
2. Sun and show-ers aid thee now, Scat-ter seed, ... With thy
3. Tho' thy work should seem to fail, Scat-ter seed, ... Hon-est

Scat-ter seed,

midst of toil and strife, Scatter seed!   Small may be thy spir-it field,
hand up-on the plow, Scatter seed!   Who can tell where grain may grow!
purpose will a-vail, Scatter seed!   Some may fall on stony ground:

Scat-ter seed!

D. S.—furrows of thy life, Scatter seed!   Small may be thy spirit field,

FINE.

But a good-ly crop 'twill yield, Sow the kindly word and deed, Scat-ter seed.
Winds are blowing to and fro; Dai-ly good thy simple creed, Scat-ter seed.
Fruit and flow'rs are oft-en found In the clefts we lit-tle heed, Scat-ter seed.

But a good-ly crop 'twill yield, Sow the kindly word and deed, Scat-ter seed.

CHORUS.   D. S.

Scat-ter seed, ... scat-ter seed; ..... In the
Scat-ter seed of good, yes, scat-ter, scat-ter seed;

COPYRIGHT, 1890, BY CHAS. H. GABRIEL.

Scattering Precious Seed.

ev - - 'ning, Sowing the precious seed by the way......
Sowing the precious seed, by the way.

No. 197. WHO AT MY DOOR IS STANDING?

Mrs. M. B. C. Slade. Dr. A B. Everett.

1. Who at my door is stand-ing, Pa-tient-ly draw-ing near,
2. Lone-ly with-out He's stay-ing, Lone-ly with-in am I;
3. All thro' the dark hours drear-y, Knock-ing a-gain is He;
4. Door of my heart, I hast-en! Thee will I o-pen wide;

En-trance with-in de-mand-ing? Whose is the voice I hear?
While I am still de-lay-ing, Will He not pass me by?
Je-sus, art Thou not wea-ry Wait-ing so long for me?
Tho' He re-buke and chas-ten, He shall with me a-bide.

D. S.—If Thou wilt heed my call-ing, I will a-bide with Thee.

REFRAIN. D. S.

Sweet-ly the tones are fall-ing:— O-pen the door for Me!

BY PER OF R M M'INTOSH.

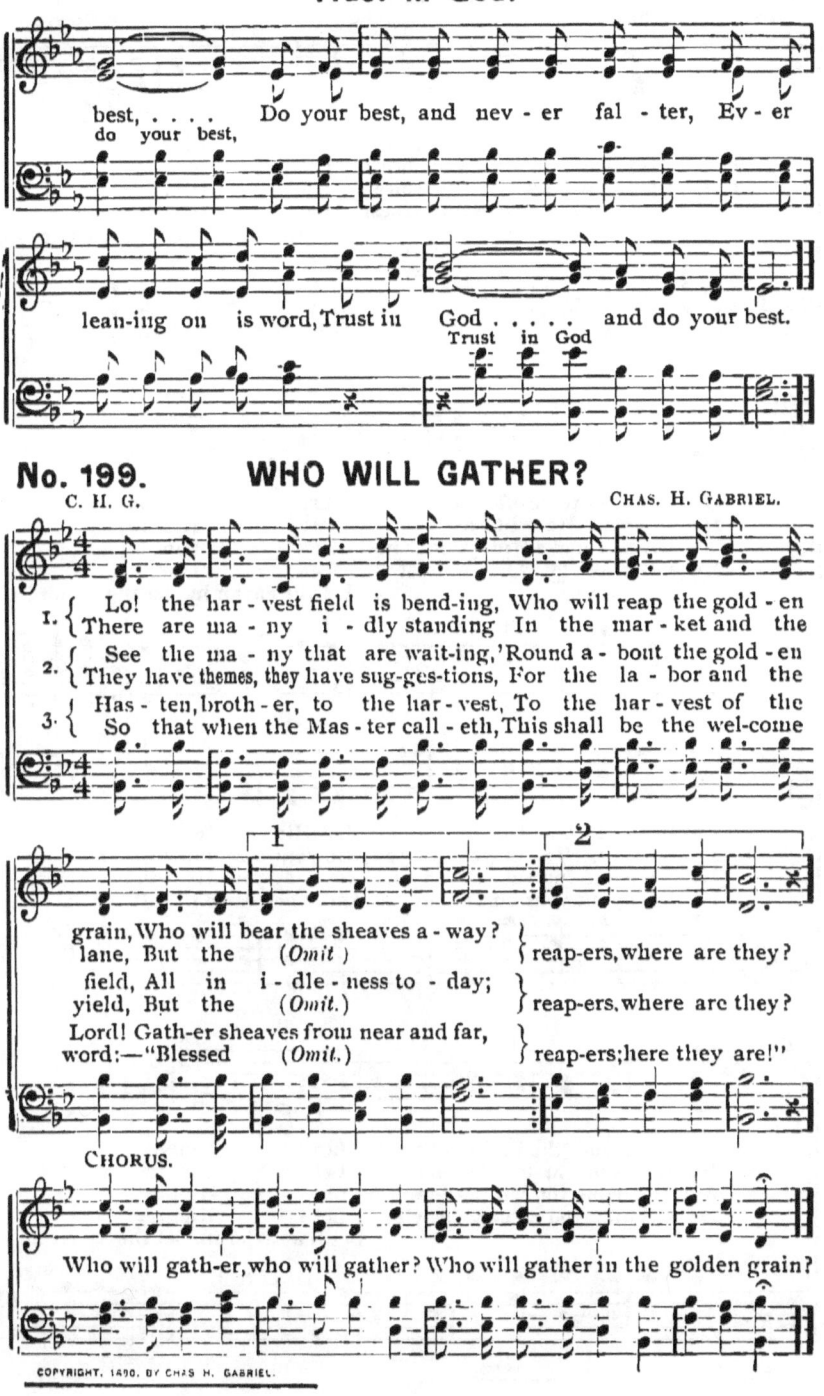

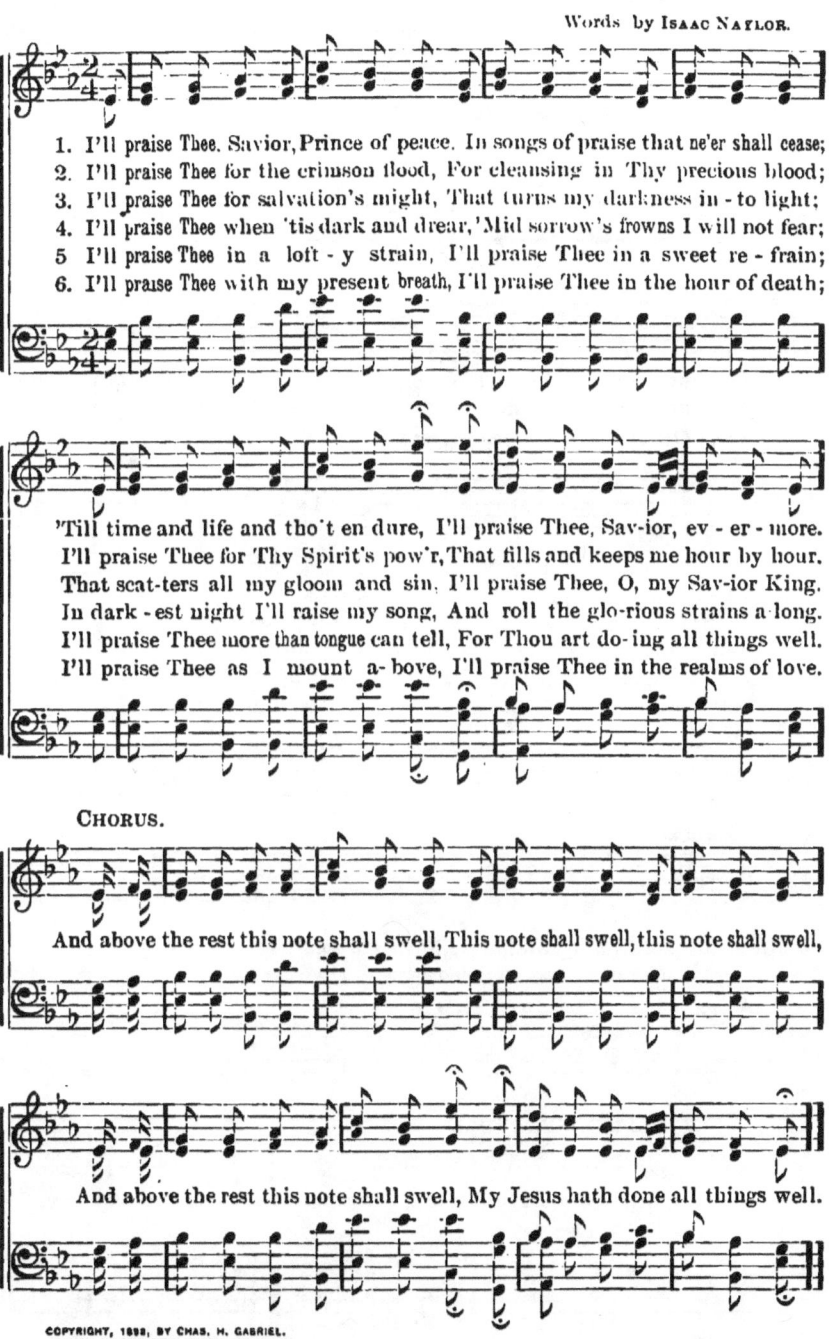

No. 207. WE ARE GOING DOWN THE VALLEY.

JESSIE H. BROWN.   J. H. FILLMORE.

1. We are go-ing down the valley, one by one, With our faces toward the
2. We are go-ing down the valley, one by one, When the la-bors of the
3. We are go-ing down the valley, one by one, Human comrade you or

set-ting of the sun;—Down the val-ley where the mournful cypress grows,
weary day are done; One by one, the cares of earth for-ev-er past,
I will there have none. But a ten-der Hand will guide us lest we fall,

CHORUS.

Where the stream of Death in si-lence onward flows. We are going down the valley,
We shall stand upon the riv-er bank at last.
Christ is go-ing down the val-ley with us all.

going down the valley, Going toward the setting of the sun; We are

going down the valley, going down the valley, Go-ing down the valley, one by one.

COPYRIGHT, 1890, BY FILLMORE BROS.

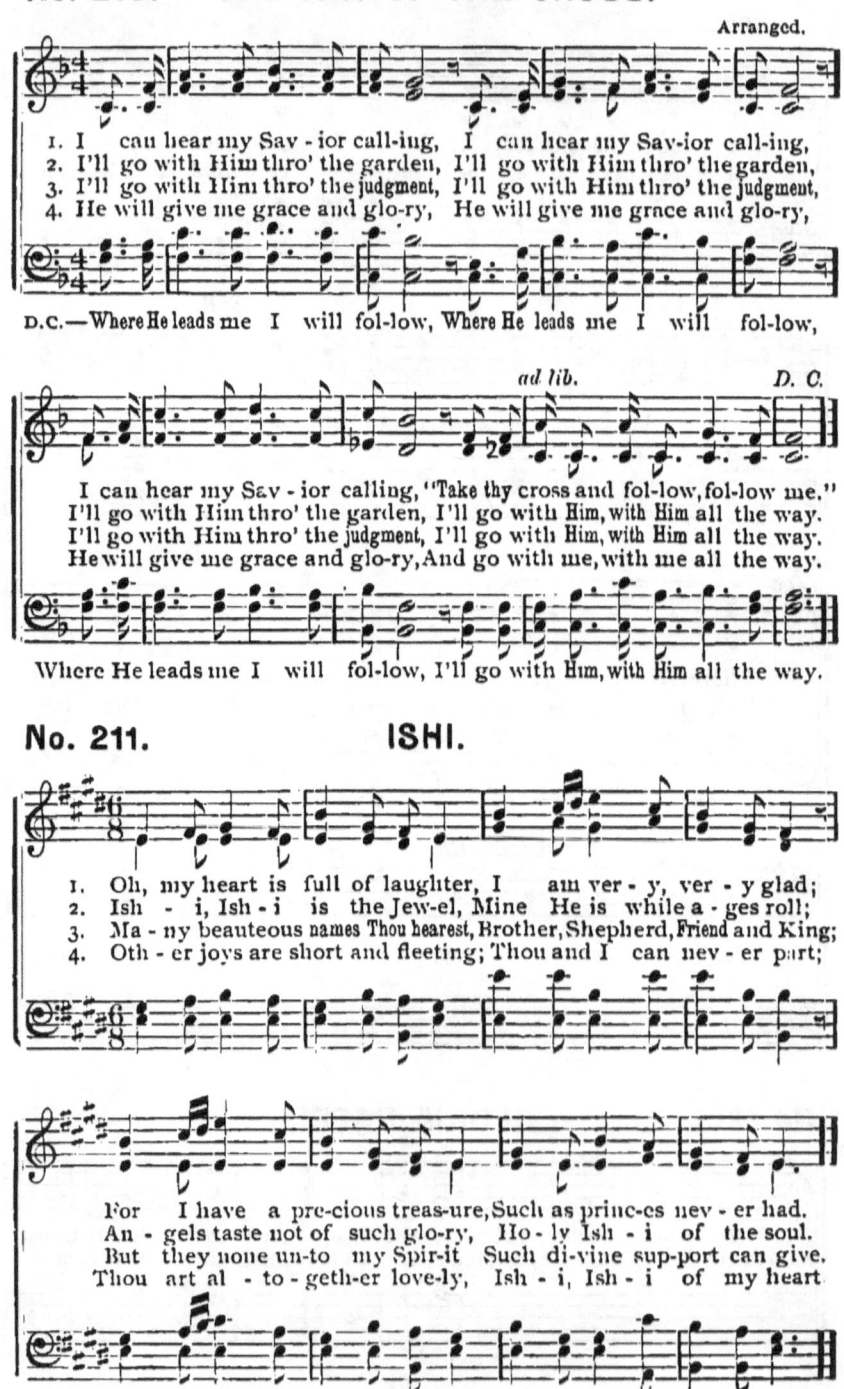

No. 214. HAPPY DAY.

P. DODDRIDGE. E. F. RIMBAULT.

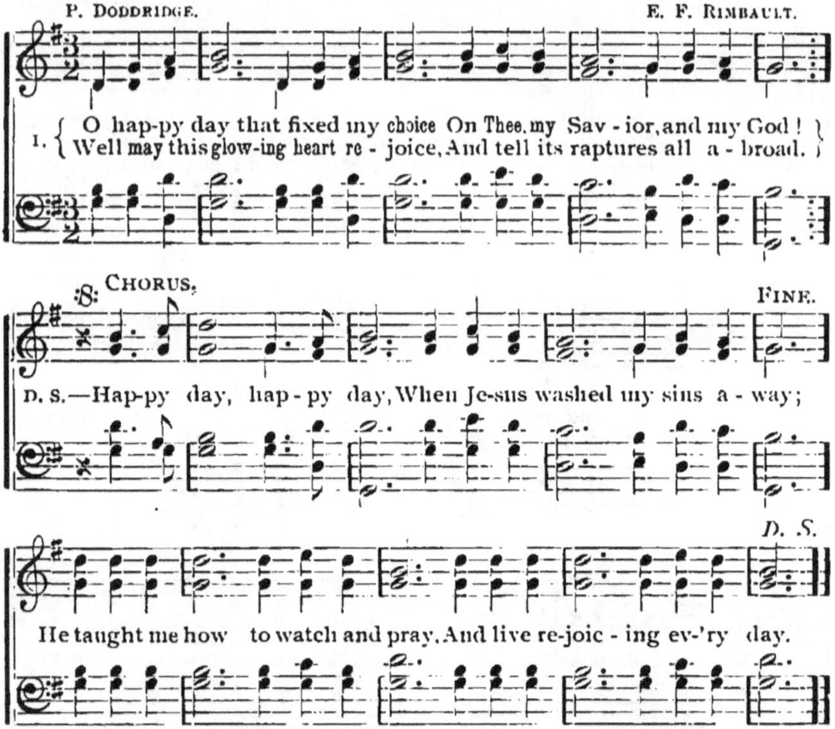

1. { O happy day that fixed my choice On Thee, my Savior, and my God! }
   { Well may this glowing heart rejoice, And tell its raptures all abroad. }

CHORUS.

D. S.—Happy day, happy day, When Jesus washed my sins away;
He taught me how to watch and pray, And live rejoicing ev'ry day.

2 O happy bond that seals my vows
  To Him who merits all my love;
  Let cheerful anthems fill His house,
  While to that sacred shrine I move.

3 'Tis done, the great transaction's done;
  I am my Lord's and He is mine;
  He drew me, and I followed on,
  Charmed to confess the voice divine.

4 Now rest, my long-divided heart,
  Fixed on this blissful centre, rest;
  Nor ever from thy Lord depart,
  With Him of every good possessed.

5 High heav'n, that heard the solemn vow,
  That vow renewed shall daily hear,
  Till in life's latest hour I bow,
  And bless in death a bond so dear.

No. 215. THE LORD'S PRAYER.

GREGORIAN.

1 Our Father which art in heaven, | Hallowed | be Thy | name. ||
   Thy kingdom come. Thy will be done in | earth, as it | is in | heaven.
2 Give us this | day our— | daily | bread. ||
   And forgive us our debts, as | we for- | give our | debtors.
3 And lead us not into temptation, but de- | liver | us from | evil: ||
   For Thine is the kingdom, and the power, and the glory, for- | ever. | A- | men.

No. 216. ROOM FOR ALL.

L. B. Bates.   C. H. G.

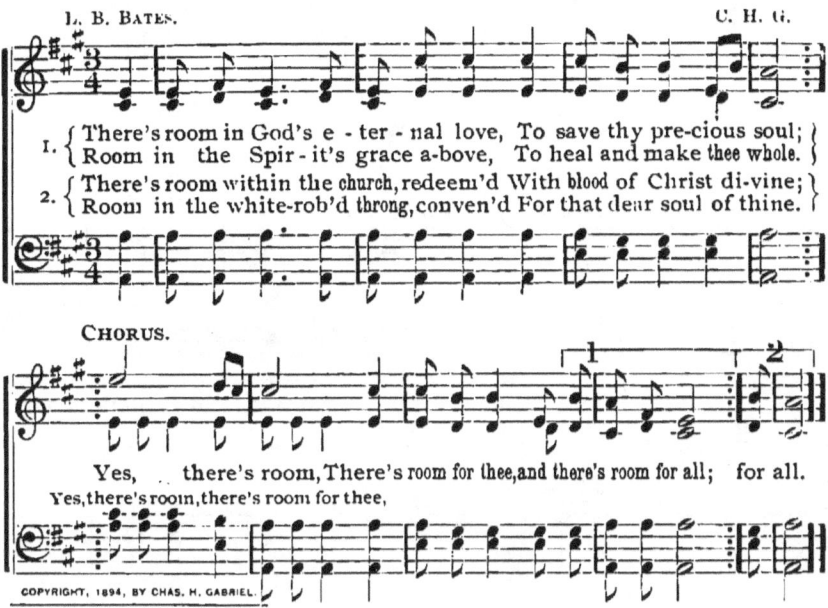

1. There's room in God's e-ter-nal love, To save thy pre-cious soul;
   Room in the Spir-it's grace a-bove, To heal and make thee whole.
2. There's room within the church, redeem'd With blood of Christ di-vine;
   Room in the white-rob'd throng, conven'd For that dear soul of thine.

CHORUS.
Yes, there's room, There's room for thee, and there's room for all; for all.
Yes, there's room, there's room for thee,

COPYRIGHT, 1894, BY CHAS. H. GABRIEL.

3 There's room in heav'n among the choir,
  And harps and crowns of gold,
  And glorious palms of vict'ry there,
  And joys that ne'er were told.

4 There's room around thy Father's board
  For thee and millions more;
  Oh, come and welcome to the Lord,
  Yea, come this very hour.

AZMON.

No. 217.

1 Oh, for a heart to praise my God,
  A heart from sin set free!
A heart that always feels Thy blood
  So freely spilt for me!

2 A heart resigned, submissive, meek,
  My great Redeemer's throne;
Where only Christ is heard to speak,
  Where Jesus reigns alone.

3 A heart in every thought renewed,
  And full of love divine;
Perfect, and right, and pure, and good,
  A copy, Lord, of Thine.

No. 218.

1 Salvation! Oh, the joyful sound!
  What pleasure to our ears;
A sovereign balm for every wound
  A cordial for our fears.

2 Salvation! let the echo fly
  The spacious earth around,
While all the armies of the sky
  Conspire to raise the sound.

3 Salvation! O Thou bleeding Lamb!
  To Thee the praise belongs;
Salvation shall inspire our hearts,
  And dwell upon our tongues.

No. 222.

1. Am I a soldier of the cross,—
   A follower of the Lamb,—
   And shall I fear to own His cause,
   Or blush to speak His name?

2. Are there no foes for me to face?
   Must I not stem the flood?
   Is this vile world a friend to grace,
   To help me on to God?

3. Sure I must fight if I would reign;
   Increase my courage. Lord!
   I'll bear the toil, endure the pain,
   Supported by Thy word.

No. 223.

1. Awake, my soul, stretch every nerve,
   And press with vigor on;
   A heavenly race demands thy zeal,
   And an immortal crown.

2. A cloud of witnesses around
   Hold thee in full survey;
   Forget the steps already trod,
   And onward urge thy way.

3. Blest Savior, introduced by Thee,
   Have I my race begun;
   And, crowned with victory. at Thy [feet
   I'll lay my honors down.

No. 224. JUST AS I AM.

CHARLOTTE ELLIOTT.   WM. BRADBURY.

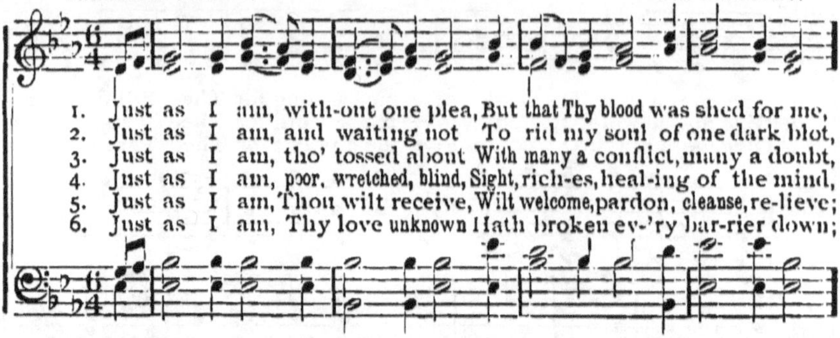

1. Just as I am, with-out one plea, But that Thy blood was shed for me,
2. Just as I am, and waiting not To rid my soul of one dark blot,
3. Just as I am, tho' tossed about With many a conflict, many a doubt,
4. Just as I am, poor, wretched, blind, Sight, rich-es, heal-ing of the mind,
5. Just as I am, Thou wilt receive, Wilt welcome, pardon, cleanse, re-lieve;
6. Just as I am, Thy love unknown Hath broken ev-'ry bar-rier down;

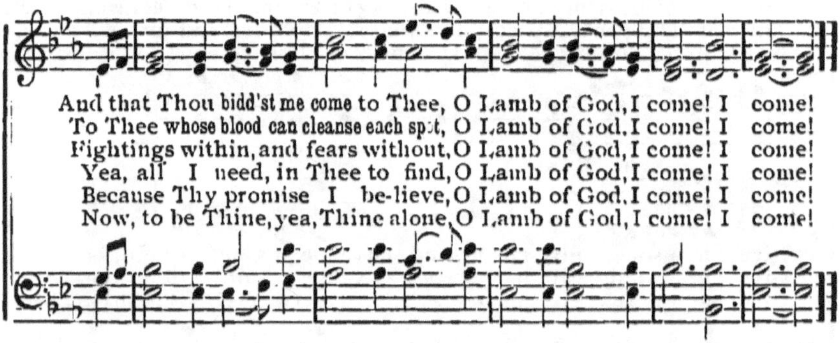

And that Thou bidd'st me come to Thee, O Lamb of God, I come! I come!
To Thee whose blood can cleanse each spot, O Lamb of God, I come! I come!
Fightings within, and fears without, O Lamb of God, I come! I come!
Yea, all I need, in Thee to find, O Lamb of God, I come! I come!
Because Thy promise I be-lieve, O Lamb of God, I come! I come!
Now, to be Thine, yea, Thine alone, O Lamb of God, I come! I come!

No. 225. CROSS AND CROWN.

THOMAS SHEPHERD.   GEO. N. ALLEN.

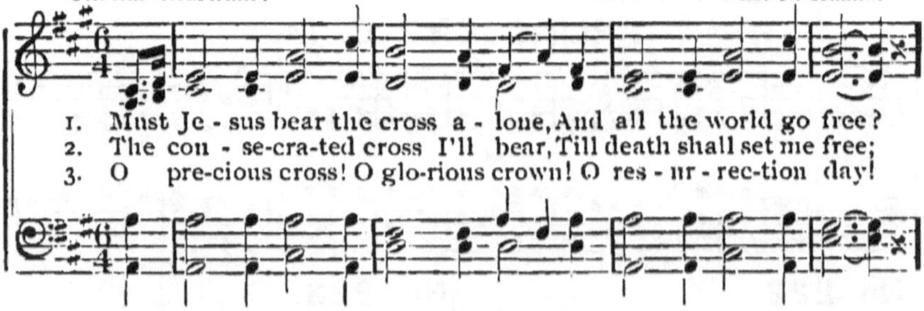

1. Must Je-sus bear the cross a-lone, And all the world go free?
2. The con-se-cra-ted cross I'll bear, Till death shall set me free;
3. O pre-cious cross! O glo-rious crown! O res-ur-rec-tion day!

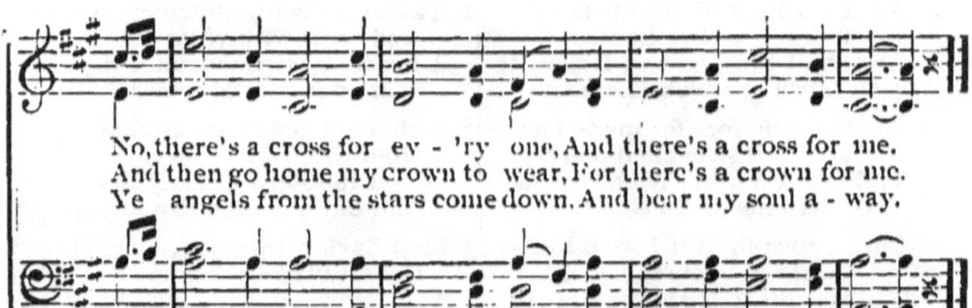

No, there's a cross for ev-'ry one, And there's a cross for me.
And then go home my crown to wear, For there's a crown for me.
Ye angels from the stars come down, And bear my soul a-way.

No. 226. WHAT A FRIEND.

H. BONAR. C. C. CONVERSE.

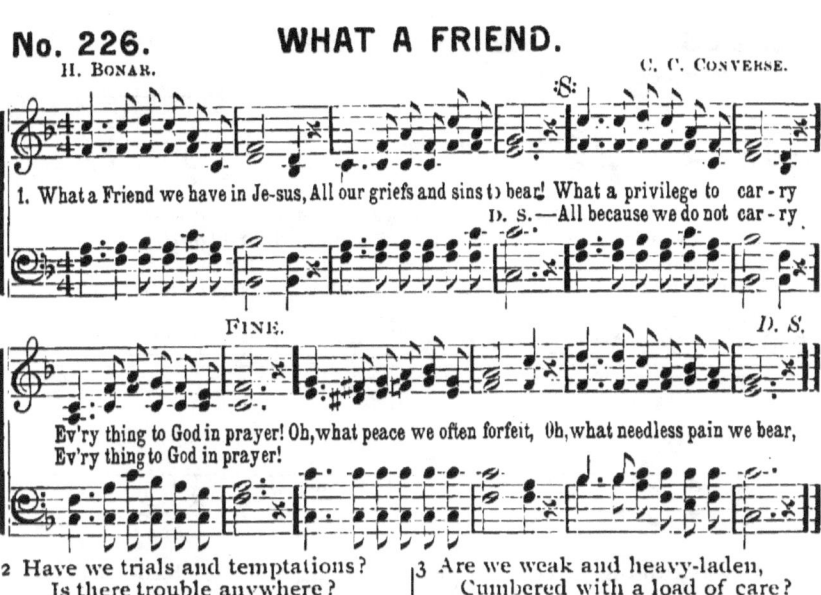

2 Have we trials and temptations?
   Is there trouble anywhere?
We should never be discouraged,
   Take it to the Lord in prayer.
Can we find a friend so faithful,
   Who will all our sorrows share?
Jesus knows our every weakness,
   Take it to the Lord in prayer.

3 Are we weak and heavy-laden,
   Cumbered with a load of care?
Precious Savior, still our refuge,—
   Take it to the Lord in prayer.
Do thy friends despise, forsake thee?
   Take it to the Lord in prayer;
In His arms He'll take and shield thee,
   Thou wilt find a solace there.

BY PERMISSION.

No. 227. COME YE THAT LOVE THE LORD.

ISAAC WATTS. Arranged.

No. 228. HE IS CALLING.

F. W. Faber.

1. { There's a wideness in God's mercy, Like the wideness of the sea;
   { There's a kindness in His justice Which is more than (*Omit.*) } lib-er-ty.
2. { There is welcome for the sinner, And more graces for the good;
   { There is mercy with the Savior, There is heal-ing (*Omit.*) } in His blood.

CHORUS.

He is call-ing, "Come to me!" Lord, I glad-ly haste to Thee.

3 For the love of God is broader
  Than the measure of man's mind;
  And the heart of the Eternal
  Is most wonderfully kind.

4 If our love were but more simple,
  We should take Him at His word;
  And our lives would be all sunshine
  In the sweetness of our Lord.

No. 229. THE GREAT PHYSICIAN.

1 The great Physician now is here,
  The sympathizing Jesus;
  He speaks the drooping heart to cheer,
  Oh, hear the voice of Jesus.

CHORUS.

Sweetest note in seraph song,
Sweetest name on mortal tongue,
Sweetest carol ever sung;
  Jesus, blessed Jesus.

2 Your many sins are all forgiven,
  Oh, hear the voice of Jesus;
  Go on your way in peace to heaven;
  And wear a crown with Jesus.

3 All glory to the dying Lamb!
  I now believe in Jesus;
  I love the blessed Savior's name,
  I love the name of Jesus.

No. 230. COME, YE SINNERS.

1 Come, ye sinners, poor and needy,
  Weak and wounded, sick and sore,
  Jesus ready stands to save you,
  Full of pity, love, and power.

CHORUS.

Turn to the Lord and seek salvation,
  Sound the praise of His dear name;
Glory, honor, and salvation,
  Christ the Lord has come to reign.

2 Now, ye needy, come and welcome,
  God's free bounty glorify;
  True relief and true repentance,
  Every grace that brings you nigh.

3 Let not conscience make you linger,
  Nor of fitness fondly dream;
  All the fitness He requireth,
  Is to feel your need of Him.

No. 231. I AM COMING TO THE CROSS.

Rev. WM. McDONALD.   WM. G. FISCHER.

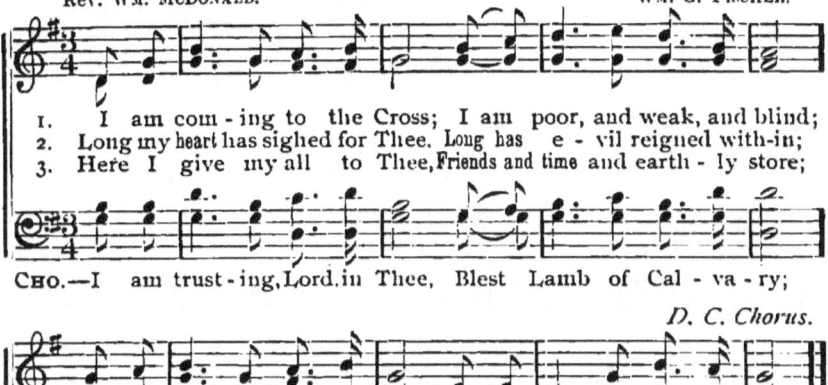

1. I am com-ing to the Cross; I am poor, and weak, and blind;
2. Long my heart has sighed for Thee, Long has e - vil reigned with-in;
3. Here I give my all to Thee, Friends and time and earth - ly store;

CHO.—I am trust-ing, Lord, in Thee, Blest Lamb of Cal - va - ry;

D. C. Chorus.

I am count-ing all but dross, I shall full sal - va - tion find.
Je - sus sweet-ly speaks to me,—"I will cleanse you from all sin."
Soul and bod - y Thine to be,—Whol-ly Thine for - ev - er - more.

Hum-bly at Thy cross I bow, Save me, Je - sus, save me now.

4 In Thy promises I trust,
   Now I feel the blood applied:
   I am prostrate in the dust,
   I with Christ am crucified.

5 Jesus comes! He fills my soul!
   Perfected in Him I am;
   I am every whit made whole:
   Glory, glory to the Lamb.

BY PERMISSION.

No. 232. MY SOUL, BE ON THY GUARD.

GEORGE HEATH.   Dr. LOWELL MASON.

1. My soul, be on thy guard; Ten thous-and foes a - rise;
2. Oh, watch, and fight, and pray, The bat - tle ne'er give o'er;
3. Ne'er think the vic - t'ry won, Nor lay thine ar - mor down,

The hosts of sin are press-ing hard To draw thee from the skies.
Re - new it bold - ly ev - 'ry day, And help di - vine im - plore.
The work of faith will not be done, Till thou ob - tain the crown.

INDEX OF TITLES.

Able and willing to save	35
Able to deliver	44
A blessing for me	78
All the way	8
All the world for Jesus	111
All thine own	143
Am I a soldier of the cross	222
Arlington	221
As a shepherd	160
As thy days thy strength shall be	45
At the foot of the cross	15
At the Landing	86
Awake my soul, stretch every nerve	223
Azmon	217
Beautiful home of the blest	42
Because He loves us so	131
Beneath His wing	219
Blessed assurance	41
Bright crowns	201
Bright forever	58
By faith I follow on	170
Can ye not watch one little hour	49
Can you doubt Him	17
Chime on sweet bells	11
Christ is all the world to me	117
Christ is passing by	24
Cleansing in the precious blood	31
Climbing up Zion's hill	71
Clinging to the rock	57
Come, holy Spirit	120
Come power of God	100
Come thou, O traveler	25
Come to the feast	108
Come to the crimson fountain	76
Come to Jesus	213
Come, ye sinners	230
Come ye that love the Lord	227
Consecration	163
Coronation	236
Cross and crown	225
Dear Lord, remember me	90
Death and eternity	123
Don't let the golden hour go by	166
Do you know the song	193
Draw me nearer	69-155
Draw near O Comforter	187
Enough for thee and me	159
Follow Jesus	67
For the right	37
For Thee, O Lord	221
For you and for me	99
Gather in the grain	4
Gloria Patri	209
Glorious fountain	65
Glory hallelujah	92
Glory land	147
Glory to the Lamb	178
God be with you	62
God is good	154
Going away unsaved	157
Hallelujah	33
Happy day	214
Happy in my Savior	168
He calleth for thee	122
He careth for me	84
He cares for me	7
He is calling	228
He knoweth	182
He loves them	144
He saves me	133
He saves me to-day	112
He shall gather the lambs	73
Here am I send me	74
He's the Savior of my soul	176
Hiding in the rock	145
Home over yonder	26
I am coming to the cross	231
I am that I am	152
I am the door	161
I believe it	208
I love thee	191
In that city over there	129
Ishi	211
I will tell the glad story	128
I'll bear the cross	79
I'm going home	181
I'm kneeling at the mercy seat	220
I'm not alone	68
I'm redeemed	139
Jesus hide me	212
Jesus is mighty to save	32
Jesus is passing by	115
Jesus the children's Friend	89
Jesus reigns	39
Jesus saves me now	95
Jesus will help you	140
Joy of crosecration	46
Just as I am	224
Just beyond the river	19
Keep close to Jesus	52
Keep the hallelujahs ringing	132
King of kings and Lord of lords	96
Lead me Savior	60
Leave it to Him	43
Let Him in	200
Let me in	171
Let the Savior in	151
Let Jesus hold your hand	66
Lift up your heads	175
Light divine	14
Little stars	103
Living for Christ	169
Living in Canaan	173
Living in the sunshine	135
Look and live	195
Look to Jesus	136

Index of Titles.

Love of God	97
Marching to the land above	130
Marching to Zion	174
Martyn	234
Mercy is boundless and free	64
More about Jesus	6
More like Jesus	55-204
More love to Thee	137
More love to Thee, O Christ	59
Must Jesus bear the cross	225
My cleansing	16
My faith looks up to Thee	51
My soul be on thy guard	232
Nearer home	107
Never look back	126
Not ashamed of Jesus	138
Nothing but the blood	127
O for a heart to praise	217
Oh, the blood	101
O joyful sound	149
Old Hundred	236
Once again	61
On the Rock	47
Onward christian soldier	20
Onward, upward	5
O sacred Head	102
Over in the glory-land	1
Pardoned, cleansed, redeemed	142
Praise Him	21
Praise His name	119
Press onward heirs of glory	104
Purity	63
Rest soldier, rest	148
Resting on God's promises	29
Rock of Ages	94
Rolling on	81
Room for all	216
Salvation is free	158
Salvation, O the joyful sound	218
Satisfied with Jesus	189
Savior go with me	121
Scatter golden grain	10
Scatter seed	192
Scatter precious seed	196
Scatter sunshine	2
Seeds of promise	134
Send the light	205
Seven times 'round	146
Shall we meet	183
Shout the tidings	165
Sing the love of Jesus	113
Soldiers of Christ	98
Sometime by and by	141
Sowing and reaping	53
Sunshine in the soul	80
Sweeping through the gates	186
Sweet Eden Land	48
Tell me the old, old story	206
The armies of God	93
The cross	12
The cleansing wave	77
The everlasting arms	194
The glad good news	34
The good Shepherd	181
The gospel bells	124
The great Physician	229
The harvest time is coming	190
The haven of rest	125
The Lamb of Calvary	153
The Lord was ready to save me	118
The Lord's prayer	215
The mansions yonder	75
The Maranatha cry	83
The Master is calling	50
The meeting in the air	106
The music of the kingdom	82
The Penitent's plea	116
The precious blood	30
The reason why	56
The soul's refuge	179
The stranger at the door	13
The sweet olden story	202
The very same Jesus	9
The victory	109
The water of life	22
The way of the cross	210
This lost world for Jesus	27
This note shall swell	203
There is glory in my soul	18
There is joy	177
There's a wideness in God's mercy	228
There's room on board	156
Thou thinkest, Lord, of me	23
Thou hast died for me	54
Though your sins be as scarlet	28
Through all eternity	110
Thy will be done	85
Thy kingdom come	167
Toplady	233
Triumph by and by	162
Trust in God	198
Vale of Beulah	184
Waiting, watching, working	38
Waiting for the crown	91
Wake the song of gladness	87
Walking in the King's highway	40
We are going down the valley	207
We are little soldiers	150
We are marching	105
What a friend	226
When Jesus came my way	36
When the roll is called	88
Where the shepherd leads	114
Where will you anchor	164
Who at my door is standing	197
Whosoever will	72
Who will gather	199
Who will stand for the right	185
Why I sing	3
Wondrous love	70
Will you go	172
You may if you will	180
Yon portal fair	188

www.ingramcontent.com/pod-product-compliance
Lightning Source LLC
Chambersburg PA
CBHW021844230426
43669CB00008B/1068